CLINICAL APPROACHES TO AGGRESSION AND VIOLENCE

edited by

KEVIN HOWELLS AND CLIVE HOLLIN

ISSUES IN CRIMINOLOGICAL AND LEGAL PSYCHOLOGY, NO. 12

GENERAL EDITORS: JOANNA SHAPLAND AND JONQUIL DRINKWATER

PUBLISHED BY THE BRITISH PSYCHOLOGICAL SOCIETY FOR THE DIVISION OF CRIMINOLOGICAL AND LEGAL PSYCHOLOGY, 1988

Published by The British Psychological Society
St Andrews House, 48 Princess Road East, Leicester LE1 7DR

ISBN 0 901715 84 0
ISSN 0226-6863

PREVIOUS TITLES IN THIS SERIES

No. 1 Lawyers and Psychologists - The Way Forward
Joanna Shapland

No. 2 Symposium: Broadmoor Psychology Department's 21st Birthday
D.A. Black

No. 3 Lawyers and Psychologists - Gathering and Giving Evidence
Joanna Shapland

No. 4 Mental Disorder and the Law: Effects of the New Legislation
Joanna Shapland and Tim Williams

No. 5 Decision Making in the Legal System
Joanna Shapland

No. 6 Options for the Mentally Abnormal Offender
Tim Williams, Elaine Alves and Joanna Shapland

No. 7 Legislation for Policing Today: The Police and Criminal Evidence Act
Elaine Alves and Joanna Shapland

No. 8 Sexual Assessment: Issues and Radical Alternatives
Peter Pratt

No. 9 Clinical Approaches to Criminal Behaviour
Clive Hollin and Kevin Howells

No. 10 Mental Handicap and the Law
Elaine Alves

No. 11 Psychological Evidence in Court
Gisli Gudjonsson and Jonquil Drinkwater

CONTENTS

ABOUT THE CONTRIBUTORS

DR RONALD BLACKBURN is Top Grade Clinical Psychologist at Park Lane Hospital, Liverpool. He has published extensively in the area of personality in relation to violent behaviour.

PROFESSOR ROBERT BLUGLASS is Professor of Forensic Psychiatry at the University of Birmingham. He has published widely in the area of forensic psychiatry, and the law in relation to mentally abnormal offenders. He will be the Director of the new regional forensic unit to be opened in Birmingham.

DR WILLIAM DAVIES is Head of the Psychology Department, St Andrews Hospital, Northampton. He has extensive experience in working with offenders and has published several papers in the area of violent offenders.

DR NEIL FRUDE is Lecturer in Psychology at University College, Cardiff where he is currently Head of Department. He has written a number of books and articles in the areas of child abuse and aggression.

MALCOLM GENTRY is Principal Clinical Psychologist in Rugby Health District. He worked previously at Glenthorne Youth Treatment Centre, and has wide experience of behavioural intervention with delinquents.

PROFESSOR MARTIN HERBERT is Professor of Psychology and Head of the Clinical Psychology training course at the University of Leicester. He has published widely in the area of child behaviour problems and their treatment. His particular interest is in conduct disorders and the triadic approach to treatment.

DR CLIVE HOLLIN is a Lecturer in Psychology at the University of Leicester, with special responsibility for a post-qualification course in behaviour modification. A former prison psychologist, he has published widely in the field of forensic psychology, particularly in clinical approaches to delinquency.

DR KEVIN HOWELLS is a Senior Lecturer in Clinical Psychology at the University of Birmingham, where he is Head of the MSc in Clinical Psychology. He has a wide range of clinical experience in working with offender groups, and has published extensively particularly in the fields of violence and sexual diversity.

EUGENE OSTAPIUK is Principal Clinical Psychologist and Director of Glenthorne Youth Treatment Centre. He has worked with disturbed adolescents and young offenders both in open and secure residential establishments. He was Project Leader of a community-based offender rehabilitation programme with the Shape Trust before joining Glenthorne. He has published book chapters and papers in this area.

INTRODUCTION

Kevin Howells and Clive Hollin

The papers presented in the following pages were given at a conference on 'Clinical Approaches to Aggression and Violence' at the University of Leicester in September 1985. This conference was the second in a planned series of meetings exploring the usefulness of the clinical approach to understanding and changing 'offending behaviours' of various kinds. In the context of these conferences the term 'clinical' is meant to imply not a medical model, whereby deviant behaviour is seen as pathological, but a focus on the individual, and on psychological methods of producing change. We felt that some forms of aggression and violence were amenable to a clinical psychological analysis and that such an analysis was overdue. This is not to say that all violence should be viewed in this way.

The dominant theoretical framework in contemporary clinical psychological practice is the cognitive-behavioural model. Progress has been made in a range of areas outside of criminal behaviour using cognitive-behavioural analysis. The nature of anxiety and depression, for example, has been illuminated and treatment programmes for such problems are now well established. In the first paper Dr Ronald Blackburn, a clinical psychologist working in a Special Hospital, extends cognitive-behavioural analysis to aggression and describes methods for treating anger and aggression.

Aggression and violence may occur in people who suffer from formal psychiatric disorder. Professor Robert Bluglass, a forensic psychiatrist, assesses the possible relationship between violence and psychiatric illness, covering psychopathy, organic syndromes, drugs, affective disorder schizophrenia and mental handicap.

The following three papers look at various facets of violence in relation to children and young people. Dr Neil Frude, a clinical psychologist, describes a preliminary model of physical violence towards children. Professor Martin Herbert considers aggression and violence by children and a particular approach to modification. Malcolm Gentry and Eugene Ostapiuk, both clinical psychologists, discuss the management of violence in young people in a very specific context - a secure residential treatment facility.

Finally, it has been our experience that many professionals who work with violent people are concerned not only to understand and 'treat' violence in the longer term, but also to prevent violent behaviour by clients in immediate, face-to-face situations. We were aware that there was little empirical, scientific work on which to base preventative measures but felt, nevertheless, that there is a need for concrete advice on what might be done of a practical nature to minimize the risks of being assaulted. Dr William Davies, a clinical psychologist in a secure psychiatric unit, makes some practical suggestions in the final paper.

COGNITIVE BEHAVIOURAL APPROACHES TO UNDERSTANDING AND TREATING AGGRESSION

Ronald Blackburn

I should like to begin this paper with a short story. A clinical psychologist was invited to spend the weekend at the home of a friend from student days, whom he had not seen for several years. He duly accepted the invitation and, after dinner on the first evening, he and his friend settled back to reminisce. After a while, his friend, who was not a psychologist, remarked that although he had intended a reunion for some time, there was also an ulterior motive in his invitation. 'I'm hoping that you can give me some professional advice,' he said, 'I'm very worried about my young son. He's showing sadistic tendencies. He wanders around the garden mutilating creatures, and he talks to himself a lot. I'd be grateful if you would have a look at him and tell me whether he might need treatment of some kind.' The psychologist agreed, and the next morning watched from a window as the boy played in the garden. The boy produced a penknife with which he proceeded to prod the soil until he found a worm. Whereupon he laid it out on the ground, and grimly sliced through it with his knife, muttering to himself as he did so.

I am going to defer the ending to the story for a moment, to consider how the theoretical orientation of the psychologist might influence his approach to the task with which he has been presented. If he happens to work in the forensic field, he will perhaps already be alerted by his knowledge that cruelty to animals in childhood is a significant precursor of behaviour disorder in adulthood (Hellman and Blackman, 1966). Whatever his orientation, he will probably be seeing this behaviour as rather unpleasant, somewhat unusual and quite possibly unhealthy. Of the several possible approaches the psychologist might bring, I will consider four, starting with a psychoanalytic persuasion.

The psychologist is aware that children of this age go through critical periods in their emotional attachments, and that these are sensitive to the dynamics of the family as a social system. He will probably be asking himself whether this behaviour is symptomatic of some instinctively based aggressive tensions precipitated by his relations with one or more family members. Should he perhaps ring his office and have the materials for the Object Relations Test sent to him? If he received an orthodox analytic training, he will doubtless already have definite ideas about the nature of the behaviour. After all, the worm is a rather obvious symbol. It is very likely that the boy's actions represent intense hostility towards his father.

Suppose our psychologist is a radical behaviourist, a behaviour modifier. He is quite confident that the causes of this worm-slicing behaviour have little to do with anything going on inside the boy. The aggressive behaviour has developed because it serves some function in relation to the boy's current environment. Obviously, there must be something unusual about the arrangement of the environmental contingencies. What is needed is a functional analysis. What were the antecedents of this behaviour? Is it perhaps under the discriminative control of changes in the weather? What are its consequences? Are the crucial reinforcing effects to be found in the reactions of the worm itself? Or is the consequence to be that the boy's mother will at any moment appear on the scene, and deliver the attentional behaviour which would otherwise be withheld? If he is really diligent, he will borrow paper, pencil and stopwatch, and settle down to a proper objective analysis, manipulating the relevant variables, presumably including the weather if need be.

Another possibility is that our psychologist is a second generation neo-behaviourist mediationist, in other words a behaviour therapist. He is also pretty well convinced that the behaviour is under environmental control, but that this effect is achieved through the medium of some internal emotional state. This is most likely anxiety since there aren't many others discussed in the literature. He used to believe that this emotional state was a classically conditioned response, but isn't too sure nowadays. At any rate, there is a good chance that the behaviour is reducing some emotional drive state, and the first thing to do is to establish this. The portable polygraph might help, and perhaps he should get hold of a children's Fear Survey Schedule. There are, of course, alternative hypotheses to test. Perhaps the child actually enjoys slicing up worms, and if so he will have to consider an aversive technique to deal with the problem, such as filling up the garden with worms. Alternatively, the behaviour might represent a modelling effect. Could it be that far from hating his father, as the analyst suspects, the boy actually admires him and has imitated <u>his</u> behaviour.

Our fourth psychologist belongs to the laid back school. He has been in the basic grade for 15 years but is well content with his lot. He has little time for doctrinaire debate, and survives because he is warm, empathic and genuine. Nevertheless, he too has already posed a question: what has this kid got against worms?

I should apologize to my clinical colleagues for these caricatures of their professional activities, but they are intended to bring out a serious point. Our psychologist watching the boy through the window is at first glance engaging in nothing more than passive observational behaviour. But he is actually engaged in a great deal of <u>thinking</u> behaviour. The boy's activities suggest a number of ideas or hypotheses which dictate certain courses of action on the part of the psychologist. But these hypotheses are obviously not inherent in the observed behaviour, which means something different to each of our different psychologists. They are a function of the frame of reference, the theoretical model, which each of our psychologists brings to this situation. It is the model which determines what aspects of the situation are attended to, and what further aspects will be selected for attention. To go back one step further, the fact that each psychologist has a commitment to a different model, that is a different body of propositions and accumulated knowledge, is unlikely to be simply the result of something so arbitrary as the university department he attended. Otherwise, how could he justify his commitment or claim any advantages for his model? It is probable that the model is one he has selected because it harmonizes with his already established beliefs and values about the world and himself. This seems to be what people mean when they say that psychotherapists work within the framework with which they are most comfortable (e.g. Frank, 1985).

Each of our psychologists, then, is aiming at a statement about reality, but it is a reality which is imposed or constructed on the basis of pre-existing knowledge or belief systems. Some of our psychologists might deny this. Our radical behaviourist, for example, would probably argue that he is not engaged in anything so messy as theorizing. He is simply trying to ascertain 'the facts', the 'relevant variables' of which the behaviour is a function. But given the possibility of a large number of such variables, how is he to set about selecting the promising ones without a prior theoretical assumption that they are promising? Facts do not lie around in pristine innocence waiting to be picked up. They become facts only in the context of a prior theory, and all theories are constrained by tacit beliefs and assumptions, including metaphysical assumptions about the nature of the world (Harré, 1981).

Our psychologist, in short, is not passively receiving information from the scene he is witnessing; he is actively engaged in finding and structuring meaning through his cognitive activities. Yet none of the theories our psychologist holds begins to account for his own behaviour. More immediately, none of the theories, which represent the dominant traditions of abnormal psychology, entertains the possibility that our worm-slicing boy is also a thinking person with his own models of the world which impose meaning and guide his behaviour. As far as our psychologist is concerned, our boy is quite literally engaging in 'mindless' violence. George Kelly's message that each one of us is a scientist (Kelly, 1955) is one we have been slow to grasp.

Let me finish the story. We left our psychologist witnessing an act of mutilation. By this time he was beginning to feel that there was perhaps some cause for concern, and as the boy appeared about to repeat the exercise, he quietly stepped outside to observe events more closely. Sure enough, the boy was ruthlessly cutting another worm in two. But the psychologist's concern evaporated as he overheard the boy say: 'There, now you have a friend'.

I am unable to attribute the source of this tale, which has been cited by more than one psychologist. It does, however, serve as a useful introduction to the basic theme of this paper, namely that a complete explanation of human aggression must include reference to the cognitive activities of the aggressor, including goals, interpretations, thoughts and meanings attached to violent action.

To the non-psychologist, this may seem little more than a statement of the obvious, and certainly there is nothing new in this notion. Toch (1983) has recently drawn attention to the book **De Ira,** written by Seneca in the first century AD. He argues this book contains most of the concepts contained in contemporary cognitive theories of aggression, and also advocates many of their treatment techniques. But for several decades reference to thoughts, awareness or interpretations of events was a minority cult, if not a heresy in the psychology of aggression, finding its main refuge in social psychology. As I have attempted to indicate, traditional models within clinical psychology have ignored and even denied the impact of cognitive processes on aggressive behaviour, and my concern here will be to indicate some of the ways in which the balance is being redressed. I should emphasize that there is currently no unitary cognitive approach to violence and what I shall describe is a loose and necessarily idiosyncratic integration of ideas from several sources, mainly from social psychology, personality theory, and cognitive behaviour modification.

Defining aggression

So far I have used the terms violence and aggressive behaviour as synonymous, but some definitions are in order at this point. In everyday usage, violence denotes the threat or application of force which has physically harmful consequences. Aggression is used rather more broadly to include any behaviour involving harm, physical or psychological. Violence sometimes implies vigorous action, but this is not necessarily the case. Pulling the trigger of a gun involves less vigour than striking a blow or thrusting a knife, but its consequences are no less injurious. There is also a more specific connotation of social undesirability in the word violence, but what we identify as aggressive is equally contaminated by social evaluations. I shall therefore continue to use these terms interchangeably.

Definitions, like facts, do not emerge in a theory-free vacuum, and most applications of the term aggression carry certain assumptions about the actions of the aggressor. We imply intent, otherwise we would not be able to distinguish aggression from accidental injury. We also imply malevolence, otherwise we would have to include behaviour such as that of the surgeon, who inflicts bodily injury for benevolent purposes. Witness also the behaviour of our worm-slicing boy. We also include under the rubric of violence attempts at injury which are unsuccessful, for example when a bomb is planted but fails to detonate. Once we accept that aggression implies malevolent and intended behaviour, then to focus on physical injury alone is rather arbitrary. Some psychologists therefore prefer to conceptualize aggression in the broader context of coercive or punitively motivated behaviour (for example, Tedeschi et al., 1974). The merit of this proposal is that it directs attention to a variety of acts which are functionally equivalent in terms of the purposes they serve. For example, from the point of view of a father, leaving a deviant son out of his will may achieve much the same effect as giving him a thrashing. This is not merely a semantic issue. As I shall argue later, the habitually violent person appears to be someone who has punitive goals which dictate coercive solutions, of which physical aggression is but one.

This broad concept of aggression as social coercion has not been widely adopted, but there is nevertheless some degree of consensus among psychologists that the term aggression is most usefully confined to behaviour which is intentionally injurious or harmful and which is directed against a person who is motivated to avoid it (Baron, 1977; Zillmann, 1979). However, intentional harm is not necessarily the primary goal of an aggressor, and a widely accepted distinction is that between angry, or annoyance-motivated aggression, in which injury to the victim serves the function of reducing an aversive emotional state; and instrumental, or incentive-motivated aggression, which facilitates some other goal (Buss, 1961; Zillman, 1979). The robber who strikes a security guard who has refused to surrender his keys, for example, is not necessarily angry, his goal being to obtain access to the money in the guard's care. Nor is he necessarily hostile towards his victim.

This distinction therefore underscores the relative independence of aggression from anger, which is generally construed as an emotional state with physiological, cognitive and expressive aspects. People may express intense displeasure by raising their voice or banging a table, but this is not a necessary precursor of aggressive behaviour. Although the weight of research evidence is that anger increases the likelihood of aggression (Rule and Nesdale, 1976), a state of anger may have a variety of consequences, such as avoidance or even self-punishment. Similarly hostility, which I shall regard here as the negative evaluation of others as conveyed in such terms as dislike, resentment or distrust (Buss, 1961) is not a necessary accompaniment of anger or aggression. Much criminal violence, then, may well be incentive-motivated. However, the kinds of violence of concern to mental health workers, such as murder, rape, child-battering or impulsive attacks which appear to have minimal provocation, are probably for the most part instances of angry aggression.

Explanations of aggression

An adequate psychological account of aggression must address three issues: (a) how does it originate? (b) how is it provoked or instigated? (c) how is it maintained and regulated? Attempts to answer these questions have been traditionally influenced by a biological conception of human aggression. Apart from some psychoanalysts and the 'pop' ethologists such as Lorenz (1966), few have seriously entertained the notion of a human aggressive instinct. Most investigators have accepted that both the provocation to aggression and the form of the response are at least partly under the control of individual learning experiences. However, many still see phylogenetic continuity in the anatomy and physiology of the vertebrate nervous system as paralleled by a similar continuity in the biological determination of aggression. In these terms, aggression is instigated by events which thwart the attainment of our needs or which threaten danger, although through human learning these may take the form of social threats such as an insult in addition to life-threatening attacks. Aggression is mediated by physiological mechanisms which provide an energizing and even directing drive state, and it is regulated by the extent to which its consequences effectively relieve the threat or incapacitate an attacker.

The most extreme biological view is that there are built-in mechanisms in the deep part of the temporal lobe which, when activatd by an appropriate stimulus, trigger full-blown, directed aggressive behaviour (Moyer, 1981). Some American psychiatrists and neurologists believe that as a result of often undetected brain pathology in this area, many violent people are the victims of a 'dyscontrol syndrome', in which spontaneous neural firing in the affected area produces involuntary outbursts of violence (Mark and Ervin, 1970; Monroe, 1978). Not unexpectedly, these investigators view violence as essentially a symptom of pathology. However, research involving brain stimulation, brain surgery, and clinical studies of those with temporal lobe abnormalities has failed to produce any firm evidence of a 'hard-wired' system mediating human aggression (Blackburn, 1984a). While violent populations typically contain a high proportion of individuals showing organic or neuropsychological deficits, recent evidence suggests that the contribution of brain pathology to violence is indirect and non-specific (Mungas, 1983).

There are, of course, some unlearned components in aggression, but these seem to be mainly to do with the arousal and expression of anger. For example, bodily expressions of rage appear very early in human development, and in so far as arousal of the sympathetic nervous system is a necessary (though not sufficient) condition for the experience of anger and other negative emotions, there may be some unlearned connection between physiological arousal and the perception of threat. Some evidence has suggested that there is a specific physiological pattern in a state of anger (see Blackburn, 1980), but this has not been a consistent finding. A widely held view is that anger involves a non-specific state of sympathetic arousal, to which we have learned to attach the label of anger on the basis of our perception of the situation (Konecni, 1975; Schachter, 1964).

One implication of a biological perspective on aggression is that human violence is an unfortunate hangover from our animal ancestry. Mark and Ervin

(1970) consider violence to be 'unwarranted and unprovoked behaviour'. However, this is a value judgement, and ignores the functions which aggression serves for an aggressor. It also ignores the fact that most human aggression serves specifically human purposes. For example, the use of tools to assist offensive aggression, the killing of other species for purposes other than obtaining food, and the capacity to bear grudges and delay revenge are all uniquely human (Tedeschi et al., 1974; Zillmann, 1979). Contrary to the biological viewpoint, some anthropologists suggest that early man was probably quite peaceable, and that we should look to cultural evolution and individual development to understand human aggression (Barnett, 1977). Increasingly, then, psychologists have come to focus on the particularly human aspects of human aggression, and this is represented most prominently in the social learning theory of Bandura (1973).

Cognitive conceptions of anger and aggression

Social learning theory is distinguished by its emphasis on human symbolic and linguistic capacities, and by the assumption that human development is largely the product of learning in a social context. For Bandura, aggression is not an unfortunate biological residual, but rather one form of coping with environmental demands acquired because of its utility in attaining rewards or eliminating annoyance. Reinforcing and punishing contingencies within the environment provide the basis for such learning, but one of Bandura's significant contributions has been to demonstrate the role of learning through observing the behaviour of a model. The vicarious experience of observing a reward for aggression may in fact be as powerful in strengthening such behaviour as actual experience.

Observational learning, however, is not a passive process, and the extent to which modelled behaviour is imitated is determined by such factors as the degree of emotional experience entailed in observing the effects of a model's behaviour, and the observer's own judgements about the equity or otherwise of the behavioural consequences. The effect of modelling is that people come to anticipate certain consequences, and their expectations or beliefs about probable outcomes can exert a more powerful control over their behaviour than the contingencies which actually obtain in the environment. Whether or not a person exhibits aggressive behaviour is, therefore, dependent on cognitive processes of anticipation or expectation of the outcome of a particular course of action. At the same time, it is recognized that the individual can engage in contemplation about the effects of alternative behaviours. Bandura also gives particular weight to the consequences which accrue to the self, and it is assumed that people are motivated to engage in behaviour which will match and not violate their standards or personal norms.

Behaviour is, therefore, seen as subject to self-regulation through processes of self-reward and self-punishment. In this respect, personal pride can be seen as a primary motivation of aggression. Conversely, as Bandura puts it, 'There is no more devastating punishment than self-contempt'. In short, having learned through a combination of direct and vicarious experiences that certain behaviours are effective in alleviating threat or gaining desired outcomes, people will subsequently execute those behaviours according to the judged effects of the behaviours on the environment and on self-esteem or respect. However, Bandura notes that it is common for self-punishment to be overridden by self-deceptive manoeuvres which justify the harmful effects of our own behaviour. Cognitive distortions in the form of dehumanizing the victim, blaming the victim, or minimizing the consequences may therefore enable us to engage in punitive actions we would otherwise condemn.

Hence social learning theory stresses the role of cognitive mediation in the regulation of aggression, and Bandura supports this model with a considerable amount of experimental data (Bandura, 1973; 1978). Cognitive mediation is also apparent in the way in which we can mitigate the harmful effects of the behaviour of others. For example, it was shown in one early study that frustration tends to produce an aggressive reaction, but not if the person judges the frustration to be justified (Pastore, 1952). Similarly, the availability of punishment can serve to inhibit people from aggression, but only if it is perceived to be legitimate (Zillman, 1979). A punishment which is seen as unjust is more likely to elicit an angry response. Also, the effect of punishment is dependent on whether or not it is an expected outcome. It has been shown, for example, that young delinquents judge the probability of apprehension for a crime to be low (Claster, 1967).

While this model implies that aggression and other forms of coping are subject to processes of reasoning, this does not mean that the products of these processes are rational in any objective sense, since all human judgement is influenced by biases to a greater or lesser extent. There may also be limits on the cognitive guidance of aggression. Zillman (1979) has proposed that limits are set by the level of physiological arousal. He suggests that cognitive mediation overrides external contingencies at moderate levels of arousal. At more extreme levels of arousal, cognitive mediation is diminished, and aggressive behaviour is then governed largely by the immediate external contingencies. Zillman suggests that impulsive violence, the so-called 'short-fuse', is a reflection of this. There is clear support for the idea that high and low levels of arousal have the effect of incapacitating cognitive judgements about the consequences of aggressive behaviour (Zillman, 1979). Similar effects may obtain in the case of some kinds of brain damage and in alcohol intoxication (Zeichner and Pihl, 1979), which correlate highly with violent crime.

Zillman's theory has an obvious attraction. Certainly it is a common experience that in an extreme state of anger people become impervious to verbal argument. However, to distinguish cognition and physiological arousal in this way is a residue of our positivist language. What we refer to as cognitions do not have a life of their own outside the brain which produces them. To talk of a relation between cognition and arousal therefore reduces to a statement about relations between different brain systems, and in this respect Zillman's appeal to a unitary concept of arousal is simplistic, as well as being inconsistent with current psychophysiology. Be that as it may, the notion that cognitive control diminishes during an emotional state has obvious implications for any treatment strategy which aims to reduce aggression by changing cognitions.

I have sketched the social learning approach to the acquisition and regulation of aggression. The relation between cognition and emotion is a central issue when we consider the instigation of aggression. Bandura gives no special treatment to anger. He sees the distinction between angry and instrumental aggression as unnecessary on the grounds that all aggression is instrumental in gaining a desired outcome. His model specifies that both aversive experiences and positive incentives produce a general increase in emotional arousal, which then motivates whatever behaviour in one's repertoire is the strongest or prepotent. Even in the face of aversive experiences, aggression is only one of a number of possible coping strategies, which might include constructive problem-solving, social withdrawal, help-seeking or turning to drink. However, as I have noted, the evidence favours a special link between anger and aggression, and I will therefore focus on the antecedents of angry aggression.

The aversive events which Bandura describes as the antecedents of an increase in emotional arousal are those which others have described as most prominent in provoking anger, and under this general heading Bandura lists physical attack, verbal attack in the form of threats or insults, and reductions in anticipated reinforcers. Novaco (1978), who has been responsible for a recent revival of interest in anger, refers to the same events but adds the category of inequity. The role of perceived equity in social interaction has received quite a lot of attention from social psychologists, but its clinical implications have been neglected. I will simply note here my impression that in an institutional setting the perception of unfairness or injustice is a common precipitator of anger arousal and conflict.

It should be stressed that with the possible exception of physical attack, which is probably not the most frequent antecedent of angry aggression, these events are aversive to the extent that the person evaluates or appraises them as such. Many instances can be identified by others as aversive on the basis of agreed social norms, but of greater importance from a cognitive perspective are the personal norms or meanings attaching to an event. Zillman notes that many acts of antisocial violence, such as murder or child abuse, appear to be preceded by quite trivial events which is why they are labelled as impulsive. However, their triviality lies in our perception of them, not those of the aggressor.

Is there, then, some common feature to these aversive events which determines the arousal of anger rather than some other state, such as anxiety or depression? First, social learning theory suggests that the cognitive appraisal of aversiveness entails an expectation of harmful consequences. For example, an insult which is not responded to may threaten further mistreatment or may leave our social status damaged. Feshbach (1970) suggests that an insult if accepted would lower self-esteem and that retaliation serves the purpose of restoring self-esteem. Toch's observations of violent people (Toch, 1969) also suggest that aggressive encounters are commonly a means of promoting or defending a self-image. He notes that in violent encounters between police and delinquents, threats to reputation or masculine status figure prominently. The anticipation of consequences harmful to some aspect of the self-concept may therefore be critical in many instances of anger arousal. However, it should be noted that in social learning theory the self-concept is not seen as some global psychic agent. Rather it is considered to be a system of cognitive structures which provide the reference mechanism or standards against which events are perceived and evaluated, and behaviour regulated (Bandura, 1978). Such cognitive structures are conceptualized as schemata, the organized knowledge accumulated in the course of experience.

The concept of the schema is an old one in psychology and has appeared in various guises in cognitive theories (e.g. Miller et al., 1960). It is one which is currently also receiving considerable attention in the developing field of social cognition (Brewer and Nakamura, 1984; Rumelhart, 1984; Taylor and Crocker, 1981; Turk and Salovey, 1985). While this work has yet to have an impact on clinical practice there is one characteristic of schemata which cognitive therapists will need to address, which is that such knowledge structures are not directly accessible to awareness, being known largely from the cognitive processes they activate. The notion that significant mediators of behaviour may be beyond conscious awareness is one which is apt to make many psychologists uncomfortable, since their own self-schemata demand that they are scientists who deal with the observable. There is, nevertheless, quite substantial evidence for unconscious processing within experimental psychology (Dixon and Henley, 1980; Meichenbaum and Gilmore, 1984). This may not, however, turn out to be much like the Freudian unconscious, which Don Bannister once likened to a dark cellar in which an old maid grapples with a sex-crazed monkey!

The arousal of anger, therefore, may entail the detection of an event which has threatening implications for our self-schemata. But threatening information can also produce anxiety or depression. What, then, determines one emotional response rather than another? Beck's theory of the relation between cognition and emotion attempts to deal with this (Beck, 1976; Beck et al., 1979). He proposes that the common categories of emotional experience are tied to the specific content of the interpretation of an event. He also employs the concept of schema, central to which is the notion of the personal domain, i.e. all the objects, whether tangible or intangible in which a person has involvement. It includes the self-concept, but also concepts of family, friends, possessions, goals and values. The nature of an emotional response is determined by whether a person perceives events as adding to, subtracting from, endangering, or impinging on his or her domain. The perception of loss, for example, results in sadness. However, in this case the loss is seen as justified or unavoidable; loss which is unjustified provokes anger. Anger, then, is aroused by the appraisal of an attack on or violation of one's domain which is judged as unwarranted. The transgression may include an assault on self-esteem, a threat to one's possessions or social attachments, or a violation of one's rights or standards. In addition blame is attributed to the offender, and for retaliation to occur the situation must not be judged as dangerous.

In Beck's theory, the course of an emotion is determined by cognitive processes in the form of basic rules or beliefs which form the basis for specific interpretations, expectancies and self-instructions. He is not very clear on whether he regards these as functions of the schemata, but we must assume, I think, that they are. However, people will not generally be immediately aware of their basic rules or assumptions. The content of their thinking as dictated by these rules takes the form of what Beck calls automatic thoughts, or what others refer to as self-statements (Meichenbaum, 1977). In the case of anger, the content is likely to focus on the injustice of the transgression, the negative attributes and intentions of the transgressor, and the need for and consequences of retaliation or corrective action. These thoughts are idiosyncratic to the person, and they are likely to be subject to bias and distortions of reality. Beck describes a number of biasing processes such as arbitrary inferences, selective abstraction, over-generalization and magnification which he has observed to be common characteristics of patients with emotional problems. Critical to his model and the treatment procedures deriving from it is the assumption that these distorted cognitions precede and are the cause of disturbing emotional states.

Although the model attempts to account for clinical disorders, it in fact provides a general model of emotion and the major concepts employed are consistent with the social learning approach to cognitive mediation. It is a rather loose theory, in which the relationships between cognitive structures, cognitive processes and the content of cognition are sometimes obscure, but several of Beck's assumptions find support in recent research on information processing. Selective attention, in which certain attributes are perceived and others ignored, is a well-established phenomenon. The tendency of people to be biased by their own rules or beliefs has been demonstrated by studies of the so called confirmatory bias, in which people recall, seek out, and attend to information which is consistent with their particular knowledge structures. Snyder (1981), for example, has demonstrated how in testing hypotheses about the attributes of another person, people consistently solicit behavioural evidence which will confirm their hypothesis and do not look for disconfirmatory data.

Everyday judgements about the frequency of events or the likelihood of particular outcomes are heavily influenced by such factors as the availability to recall of particular examples, the recency of certain experiences, or stereotypic preconceptions (see Turk and Salovey, 1985). However, Beck's assumption that faulty cognitions are the cause of strong emotional reactions is open to question, and is currently the subject of debate (Kuiper and MacDonald, 1983; Lazarus, 1984; Zajonc, 1984). Recent research by Bower (1981) has shown that the content of recall, imaginative productions and social perceptions is dependent on mood state. In this respect, it is likely that an angry person will recall previous transgressions and focus on negative attributes of a transgressor because he is in an angry mood. This may be a pseudo-issue, and it is probably more appropriate to view emotion and cognitions as reciprocally related (Kuiper and MacDonald, 1983). However, it raises questions about how changes in emotional responses can be achieved by changing faulty cognitions, which is the strategy of cognitive therapies such as that of Beck.

Violent personalities

So far I have considered how a cognitive social learning perspective aims to account for states of anger and violent behaviour as human phenomena. These are not in themselves pathological, people come to the attention of clinicians when the frequency and intensity of their angry reactions become distressing to themselves and others, and particularly when they result in damage to others. How can the problems of violent people be conceptualized in terms of this cognitive perspective?

Social learning theorists firmly reject Skinner's view that 'a person does not act upon the world; the world acts on him' (Skinner, 1971). They see a reciprocal relationship between the person as a consciously aware being, behaviour, and the environment (Bandura, 1978; Mahoney, 1977). People, in short, create their environments, but are in turn shaped by them. There is no doubt that environments vary in their capacity to generate violence, and social learning theory would predict that violence becomes more likely when people anticipate arbitrary punishments or perceive threats to expected rewards. Environments which foster such conditions are therefore more likely to produce violent reactions. Nevertheless even within such conditions many people are deterred from violence, and in society at large only a minority engage in violence to an extent which invites social concern. Some people are more prone to violence than others.

Bandura (1973) and Mischel (1968) have strongly resisted the notion that people exhibit stable personality characteristics, since social learning theory has been mainly concerned with the ways in which people change their behaviour in response to perceived situational demands. However, there is evidence that the degree of consistency or stability of behaviour has been considerably underestimated, and this evidence comes particularly from longitudinal studies of aggressive behaviour. Olweus (1979, 1981) has reviewed these studies in detail, and concludes that individual differences in aggression remain stable over many years. Farrington (1978), for example, showed that the majority of a sample of violent delinquents had already been identified as aggressive in their early years at school. The concept of violence-prone personalities therefore has a firm foundation, but such a concept is, I believe, compatible with social learning theory (Blackburn, 1983).

However, people who have exhibited serious violence are not homogeneous. Toch (1969) differentiated ten interpersonal styles among the chronically violent, which he subsumed under two broad headings: those who use violence egocentrically as a means of exploitation, and those who engage in violence as a means of defending or promoting a vulnerable self-image. In my own work with Special Hospital patients, I have identified four groups on the basis of personality characteristics (Blackburn, 1971; 1986). Two of these represent what have been described as overcontrolled personalities, that is they are people who are characteristically restrained and unaggressive and have succumbed to an act of extreme violence under stress, which may in part be self-generated (Howells, 1976; Megargree, 1966). The other two groups show some resemblance to Toch's two categories. They represent people who are more habitually violent, but one group shows self-confident and dominant behaviour, while the other group is anxious and submissive. They correspond to what have been described respectively as primary and secondary psychopaths.

I believe that the violence of these habitually aggressive people becomes more understandable when seen in the light of their preferred interpersonal style. They appear to have characteristic styles or strategies for coping with social relationships which are more likely to provoke violent encounters with others. These preferred styles are not random but represent a means of obtaining outcomes consistent with a view of the world as a hostile place (Blackburn, 1984b).

In terms of the cognitive approach I have been describing, it is possible to see the difficulties of these people in terms of deficiencies in self-regulatory processes. They readily anticipate negative and hostile outcomes in interpersonal exchanges, attribute malicious intentions to others, reward themselves for punitive solutions, and minimize their harmful behaviour with self-justificatory biased evaluations. In Beck's terms, they appear to have a bias to look for and perceive in the behaviour of others an unwarranted violation of their personal domain. Beck has argued that depressed people are dominated by negative schemata which dictate a focus on their own shortcomings. It would appear that violent people may be dominated in a similar way by schemata which bias them to focus on the negative characteristics of others. We would, therefore, expect that acts of disruption or assault would be preceded by distorted automatic thoughts or self-statements about the blameworthiness of the victims, the need for reprisals, and self-justification for harm.

Firm evidence for this picture is currently limited. A high degree of hostility is characteristic of the personality test data of our violent subjects, and we have recently shown that they are more easily aroused to anger, particularly by personal criticisms and challenges (Blackburn and Lee-Evans, 1985). We have also found some evidence for identifiable interpersonal styles in behaviour as rated by hospital staff (Blackburn and Maybury, 1985). There is in addition evidence that aggressive boys more readily attribute hostility to others in interpersonal encounters (Dodge and Newman, 1981).

In one sense, there is nothing particularly new about this. Psychotherapists have commented on the problems of trust exhibited by violent offenders (Carney, 1976), and it has been suggested that a rebellious, withdrawn style represents a fear and avoidance of intimacy (Carson, 1970). This seems to be particularly true of our secondary psychopath category. A cognitive social learning perspective, however, suggests a number of strategies for therapeutic intervention.

Cognitive-behavioural methods in the treatment of anger and aggression

I have characterized the violent person as someone who has a punitive style of thinking and behaving which originates in biased interpretations of the world as a hostile place. The approach I have outlined suggests that the appropriate targets for reducing violence are the cognitive processes which precede and accompany situations of conflict, and the biased assumptions on which these are based. It is, however, unlikely that getting the violent person to recognize these will be sufficient to change them. A cognitively oriented approach has to consider the effects of the environmental contingencies which might sustain hostile beliefs, and the provision of non-confrontational behavioural skills which may elicit less negative reactions from others, as well as attending to the biased information-processing strategies of the client.

Cognitive behaviour modification refers to a range of procedures which have in common the assumption that faulty cognitions underlie many behavioural problems, and hence correcting these is essential to changing maladaptive behaviour. While many behaviour therapy techniques incorporate cognitive elements, approaches which assume that cognitive change is itself critical to behaviour change fall under the headings of problem-solving training and cognitive restructuring. Problem-solving training entails the identification of a problem, the setting of goals, and the generation of possible solutions to the attainment of the goal (D'Zurilla and Goldfried, 1971). Cognitive restructuring includes Beck's Cognitive Therapy (Beck, 1976), Ellis's Rational-Emotive Therapy (Ellis, 1977a) and Meichenbaum's Self-Instructional Training (Meichenbaum, 1977). The common features of these methods lie in training the client to recognize maladaptive cognitions accompanying problematic behaviour and substitute alternative and more adaptive thinking. While many of these methods entail 'talking therapy' aimed at debating, challenging and invalidating faulty inferences and examining alternatives, they are also behavioural in that a range of procedures developed within behaviour therapy form an integral part of the treatment programme. Therapists therefore frequently employ role-play, modelling and skills training, and set the client behavioural tasks which will test the hypotheses represented in faulty assumptions. The process of hypothesis testing is in fact considered to be crucial to the reformulation of experience.

These procedures appear to be used increasingly by psychologists working with socially deviant populations, but to date there has been very little evaluation of their utility with aggressive people. Bornstein et al. (1981) reviewed the application of behavioural approaches to aggression. The number of reported evaluations was not extensive, and although several described beneficial effects follow-ups were rare. At that time they identified two reports of approaches incorporating cognitive restructuring procedures, and only a handful of studies have been reported since then. These have for the most part involved non-clinical and non-criminal subjects, a typical example being young children showing behaviour problems in residential settings.

The best known approach in this area is that of Novaco (1978) who has developed a programme which aims at the self-regulation of anger. He views anger as a stress response meriting attention regardless of whether or not violence is the presenting problem. His method takes account of behavioural, physiological and cognitive components of anger, and involves an adaptation of Meichenbaum's 'stress-inoculation training' procedures. There are three stages in the programme. The first is cognitive preparation. The client is introduced to the nature and functions of anger and the rationale of the programme, is given an instruction manual, and is asked to begin a diary of anger experiences both to facilitate awareness of the relation between anger and self-statements and to monitor progress. Diary incidents form a basis for examining cognitions in subsequent sessions. The conditions which elicit anger are reviewed at this stage, and training aims to help the client discriminate between justified and unjustified anger.

At the second stage, skill acquisition, the client is taught how to reappraise anger-eliciting events, to shift from a personal orientation to a task orientation in confronting difficulties, and to employ selfinstructions in the course of an angry exchange. The self-instructions are statements which guide coping attempts and which provide self-reinforcement. Relaxation training is given as a further self-control skill, and behavioural skills of communication and assertion are taught using modelling role play. The third stage is application practice, in which developing skills are applied and tested in graded simulated anger situations. The package described by Novaco can be used on an individual or a group basis.

Novaco reports an evaluation of the procedure with an outpatient group, in which the full package was shown to be more effective in reducing the frequency and intensity of anger reactions than the use of cognitive or relaxation components in isolation. He also describes a case study of anger management in a depressed patient (Novaco, 1977), and has successfully taught these procedures to police and probation officers. Modified versions of Novaco's method have been applied effectively to reducing angry reactions in child-abusing parents (Nomellini and Katz, 1983), and to reducing the violent behaviour of an institutionalized female patient with epilepsy (Bistline and Frieden, 1984). However, the utility of these methods with violent offender populations does not appear to have been evaluated as yet. In a recent comparative study using angry students, Moon and Eisler (1983) compared Novaco's method with social skills training in assertion and problem-solving training. All methods had a significant effect on anger, but the social skills and problem-solving training had the additional advantage of improving assertion.

The self-instructional training component of Novaco's procedure has been used widely to teach impulsive children greater control, and I have identified four studies in which it has been used with aggressive children (Camp et al., 1977; Feindler et al., 1984; Kettlewell and Kausch, 1983; Snyder and White, 1979). These were all concerned with more general academic or social problem solving and were effective in this regard. Only one showed a reduction in observed aggression, but as this was not a specific target in these studies it is perhaps not unexpected. The only other demonstration of the use of cognitive methods with a clinical population appears to be that of Frederiksen and Rainwater (1981), who applied a combination of cognitive restructuring and social skills training to patients exhibiting explosive violence. Of patients who completed the programme and who were followed up for between six months and four years, all had decreased violent outbursts.

Ellis has produced a self-help manual for anger problems (Ellis, 1977b), and Beck (1976) notes the application of his procedures to anger. However, no reports on its effectiveness are available. As Beck's procedures aim to go beyond automatic thoughts or self-statements to the cognitive structure from which they are assumed to arise, these would seem to hold particular promise in dealing with violent people. Nevertheless, it is clear that we have some way to go before we can claim advantages for these methods in dealing with violence.

What I have outlined is a perspective on violence rather than a solid theory. We still know very little about the cognitive processes of violent people, and some of our basic assumptions may well be incorrect. For example, recent work on depression suggests that, although patients are indeed dominated by pessimistic thoughts, their personal evaluations may actually be less distorted than those of the non-depressed (Layne, 1983). Could it perhaps be the case that the mistrust and cynicism seen commonly in violent people is actually congruent with reality, and that it is the non-violent majority who maintain their adjustment by means of a defensive illusory glow? Also, we have not yet defined the limits of cognitive therapies. If Zillman is correct in arguing that cognitive mediation disappears in extreme violence, then the best we can do is to help the aggressive person avoid reaching that stage. Finally, the cognitive therapies assume that the cognitive structures from which biased conceptions arise are in principle available to awareness. Yet they may not be. How we change these schemata remains the ultimate problem.

References

BANDURA, A. (1973) **Aggression: A Social Learning Analysis.** Englewood Cliffs, NJ: Prentice Hall

BANDURA, A. (1978) The self in reciprocal determinism. **American Psychologist, 33,** 344-358

BARNETT, A. (1977) Ethology and man: science or myth? **Developmental Medicine and Child Neurology, 19,** 252-264

BARON, R.A. (1977) **Human Aggression.** New York: Plenum

BECK, A.T. (1976) **Cognitive Therapy and the Emotional Disorders.** New York: International Universities Press

BECK, A.T., RUSH, A.J., SHAW, B.F. and EMERY, G. (1979) **Cognitive Therapy of Depression.** Chichester: Wiley

BISTLINE, J.L. and FRIEDEN, F.P. (1984) Anger control: a case study of a stress inoculation treatment for a chronic aggressive patient. **Cognitive Therapy and Research, 8,** 551-556

BLACKBURN, R. (1971) Personality types among abnormal homicides. **British Journal of Criminology, 11,** 14-31

BLACKBURN, R. (1980) Aggression (physiological). In: R.H. Woody (ed.) **Encyclopedia of Clinical Assessment.** San Francisco: Jossey Bass

BLACKBURN, R. (1983) Psychometrics and personality theory in relation to dangerousness. In: J. Hinton (ed.) **Dangerousness: Problems of assessment and prediction.** London: Allen & Unwin

BLACKBURN, R. (1984a) The neurophysiology of violence. Paper presented at a conference on 'The Role of the Doctor in a Violent Society', London

BLACKBURN, R. (1984b) A cognitive approach to antisocial personality: implications for theory and therapy. Paper presented at a conference on 'The Mentally Disordered Offender: Issues in treatment and rehabilitation', Park Lane Hospital, Liverpool

BLACKBURN, R. (1986) Patterns of personality deviation among violent offenders. **British Journal of Criminology, 26,** 254-269

BLACKBURN, R. and LEE-EVANS, J.M. (1985) Reactions of primary and secondary psychopaths to anger evoking situations. **British Journal of Clinical Psychology, 24,** 93-100

BLACKBURN, R. and MAYBURY, C. (1985) Identifying the psychopath: the relation of Cleckley's criteria to the interpersonal domain. **Personality and Individual Differences, 6,** 375-386

BORNSTEIN, P.H., HAMILTON, S.B. and McFALL, M.E. (1981) Modification of adult aggression: a critical review of theory, research and practice. In: M. Hersen, R.M. Eisler and P.M. Miller (eds) **Progress in Behaviour Modification,** Volume 12. New York: Academic Press

BOWER, G.H. (1981) Mood and memory. **American Psychologist, 36,** 129-145

BREWER, W.F. and NAKAMURA, G.V. (1984) The nature and functions of schemas. In: R.S. Wyer and T.K. Srull (eds) **Handbook of Social Cognition,** Volume 1. Hillsdale, NJ: Erlbaum

BUSS, A.H. (1961) **The Psychology of Aggression.** New York: Wiley

CAMP, B.W., BLOM, G.E., HERBERT, F. and VAN DOORNINCK, W.J. (1977) 'Think Aloud': a program for developing self-control in young aggressive boys. **Journal of Abnormal Child Psychology, 5,** 157-169

CARNEY, F.L. (1976) Treatment of the aggressive patient. In: D.J. Madden and J.T. Lion (eds) **Rage, Hate, Assault and Other Forms of Violence.** New York: Spectrum

CARSON, R.C. (1970) **Interaction Concepts of Personality.** London: Allen & Unwin

CLASTER, D.S. (1967) Comparison of risk perception between delinquents and non-delinquents. **Journal of Criminal Law, Criminology and Police Science, 58,** 80-86

DIXON, N.F. and HENLEY, S.H.A. (1980) Without awareness. In: M. Jeeves (ed.) **Psychology Survey No. 3.** London: Allen & Unwin

DODGE, K.A. and NEWMAN, J.P. (1981) Biased decision-making processes in aggressive boys. **Journal of Abnormal Psychology, 90,** 375-379

D'ZURILLA, T. and GOLDFRIED, M. (1971) Problem solving and behaviour modification. **Journal of Abnormal Psychology, 78,** 107-126

ELLIS, A. (1977a) The basic clinical theory of Rational-Emotive Therapy. In: A. Ellis and R. Grieger (eds) **Handbook of Rational-Emotive Therapy.** New York: Springer

ELLIS, A. (1977b) **How to Live With - and Without - Anger.** New York: Reader's Digest Press

FARRINGTON, D.P. (1978) The family backgrounds of aggressive youths. In: L. Hersov, M. Berger and D. Schaffer (eds) **Aggression and Antisocial Disorder in Children.** London: Pergamon

FEINDLER, E.L., MARRIOTT, S.A. and IWATA, M. (1984) Group anger control training for junior high school delinquents. **Cognitive Therapy and Research, 8,** 299-311

FESHBACH, S. (1970) Aggression. In: P.H. Mussen (ed.) **Carmichael's Manual of Child Psychology,** Volume 2. New York: Wiley

FRANK, J.D. (1985) Therapeutic components shared by all psychotherapies. In: M.J. Mahoney and A. Freeman (eds) **Cognition and Psychotherapy.** New York: Plenum

FREDERIKSEN, L.W. and RAINWATER, N. (1981) Explosive behaviour: a skill development approach to treatment. In: R.B. Stuart (ed.) **Violent Behaviour: Social learning approaches to prediction,management and treatment.** New York: Brunner/Mazel

HARRÉ, R. (1981) The positivist-empiricist approach and its alternatives. In: P. Reason and J. Rowan (eds) **Human Inquiry.** Chichester: Wiley

HELLMAN, D.S. and BLACKMAN, W. (1966) Enuresis, firesetting and cruelty to animals: a triad predictive of adult crime. **American Journal of Psychiatry, 122,** 1431-1435

HOWELLS, K. (1976) Interpersonal aggression. **International Journal of Criminology and Penology, 4,** 319-330

KELLY, G.A. (1955) **The Psychology of Personal Constructs.** New York: Norton

KETTLEWELL, P.W. and KAUSCH, D.F. (1983) The generalization of the effects of a cognitive-behavioural treatment program for aggressive children. **Journal of Abnormal Child Psychology, 11,** 101-114

KONECNI, V.J. (1975) The mediation of aggressive behaviour: arousal level versus anger and cognitive labelling. **Journal of Personality and Social Psychology, 32,** 706-712

KUIPER, N.A. and MACDONALD, M.R. (1983) Reason, emotion, and cognitive therapy. **Clinical Psychology Review, 3,** 297-316

LAYNE, C. (1983) Painful truths about depressives' cognitions. **Journal of Clinical Psychology, 39,** 848-853

LAZARUS, R.S. (1984) On the primacy of cognition. **American Psychologist, 39,** 124-129

LORENZ, K. (1966) **On Aggression.** London: Methuen

MAHONEY, J.J. (1977) Reflections on the cognitive-learning trend in psychotherapy. **American Psychologist, 32,** 5-13

MARK, V.H. & ERVIN, F.R. (1970) **Violence and the Brain.** New York: Harper & Row

MEGARGEE, E.I. (1966) Undercontrolled and overcontrolled personality types in extreme antisocial aggression. **Psychological Monographs, 80,** Whole No. 611

MEICHENBAUM, D. (1977) **Cognitive-Behaviour Modification.** New York: Plenum

MEICHENBAUM, D. and GILMORE, J.B. (1984) The nature of unconscious processes: a cognitive behavioural perspective. In: K.S. Bowers and D. Meichenbaum (eds) **The Unconscious Reconsidered.** New York: Wiley

MILLER, G.A., GALANTER, E. and PRIBRAM, K.H. (1960) **Plans and Structure of Behaviour.** New York: Holt, Rinehart & Winston

MISCHEL, W. (1968) **Personality and Assessment.** New York: Wiley

MONROE, R. (1978) **Brain Dysfunction in Aggressive Criminals.** Lexington, Mass: Heath

MOON, J.R. and EISLER, R.M. (1983) Anger control: an experimental comparison of three behavioural treatments. **Behaviour Therapy, 14,** 493-505

MOYER, K.E. (1981) Biological substrates of aggression and implications for control. In: P.F. Brain and D. Benton (eds) **The Biology of Aggression.** Alphen aander Rijn: Sijthoff & Noordhoff

MUNGAS, D. (1983) An empirical analysis of specific syndromes of violent behaviour. **Journal of Nervous and Mental Disease, 171,** 354-361

NOMELLINI, S. and KATZ, R.C. (1983) Effects of anger control training on abusive parents. **Cognitive Therapy and Research, 7,** 57-68

NOVACO, R.W. (1977) Stress inoculation: a cognitive therapy for anger and its application to a case of depression. **Journal of Consulting and Clinical Psychology, 45,** 600-608

NOVACO, R.W. (1978) Anger and coping with stress. In: J.P. Foreyt and D.P. Rathjen (eds) **Cognitive Behaviour Therapy.** New York: Plenum

OLWEUS, D. (1979) Stability of aggressive reaction patterns in males: a review. **Psychological Bulletin, 86,** 852-875

OLWEUS, D. (1981) Continuity in aggressive and withdrawn inhibited patterns. **Psychiatry and Social Science, 1,** 141-159

PASTORE, N. (1952) The role of arbitrariness in the frustration-aggression hypothesis. **Journal of Abnormal and Social Psychology, 47,** 728-731

RULE, B.G. and NESDALE, A.R. (1976) Emotional arousal and aggressive behaviour. **Psychological Bulletin, 83,** 851-863

RUMELHART, D.E. (1984) Schemata and the cognitive system. In: R.S. Wyer and T.K. Srull (eds) **Handbook of Social Cognition,** Volume 1. Hillsdale, NJ: Erlbaum

SCHACHTER, S. (1964) The interaction of cognitive and physiological determinants of emotional state. In: L. Berkowitz (ed.) **Advances in Experimental Social Psychology,** Volume 1. New York: Academic Press

SKINNER, B.F. (1971) **Beyond Freedom and Dignity.** Harmondsworth: Penguin

SNYDER, J.J. and WHITE, M.J. (1979) The use of cognitive self-instruction in the treatment of behaviourally disturbed adolescents. **Behaviour Therapy, 10,** 227-235

SNYDER, M. (1981) Seek and ye shall find: testing hypotheses about other people. In: E. Higgins, C. Herman and M. Zanna (eds) **Social Cognition: The Ontario Symposium.** Hillsdale, NJ: Erlbaum

TAYLOR, S.E. and CROCKER, J. (1981) Schematic bases of social information processing. In: E.T. Higgins, C.P. Herman and M.P. Zanna (eds) **Social Cognition: The Ontario Symposium.** Hillsdale, NJ: Erlbaum

TEDESCHI, J.T., SMITH, R.B. and BROWN, R.C. (1974) A reinterpretation of research on aggression. **Psychological Bulletin, 81,** 540-562

TOCH, H. (1969) **Violent Men.** Harmondsworth: Penguin

TOCH, H. (1983) The management of hostile aggression: Seneca as applied social psychologist. **American Psychologist, 38,** 1022-1026

TURK, D.C. and SALOVEY, P. (1985) Cognitive structures, cognitive processes, and cognitive-behaviour modification: 1. Client issues. **Cognitive Therapy and Research, 9,** 1-17

ZAJONC, R.B. (1984) On the primacy of affect. **American Psychologist, 39,** 117-123

ZEICHNER, A. and PIHL, R.O. (1979) Effects of alcohol and behaviour contingencies on human aggression. **Journal of Abnormal Pschology, 88,** 153-160

ZILLMAN, D. (1979) **Hostility and Aggression.** Hillsdale, NJ: Erlbaum

PSYCHIATRIC APPROACHES TO AGGRESSION AND VIOLENCE

Robert Bluglass

The search for an understanding of the problem of human aggression and violent behaviour is so complex that one should hasten to limit one's contribution to remain within the boundaries of a specific approach. I am concerned with the clinical approach to this problem, but inevitably this must to some extent reflect the work of behavioural scientists, psychologists, philosophers, theologists, and the approach of the law. There is a voluminous literature which includes psychoanalytical theory, behaviourist theories based upon the notion of social learning, ethological postulates of instinctive drives, sociological theory, the contributions of physiology, genetics, neurology, biochemistry, endocrinology and psychiatry.

Violent and aggressive behaviour is so widespread and commonplace that it is difficult if not impossible to consider this form of behaviour in a single, meaningful way. Anthony Storr in his valuable work **Human Aggression** (1968) has observed that:

> 'When a word becomes so diffusely applied that it is used both as the competitive striving of a footballer and also of the bloody violence of the murderer, it ought either to be dropped or else be more closely defined.'

There can be no dispute that aggression is a normal phenomenon, an inevitable and identifiable characteristic of the behaviour not only of human beings but of most other species. It serves a wide variety of functions and is essential for survival and for the integrity of personality. As clinicians, we are concerned with maladaptive aggressive behaviour, destructive violence and cruelty. Even these behaviours are too commonplace to be explicable simply in terms of psychiatric disorder. The indiscriminate demonstration of aggression which took place during the Birmingham riots in Handsworth (Monday, 9 September 1985), for example, particularly emphasizes my point.

The importance of the wide variety of theories that I have mentioned and of economic, social and political factors in the definition and understanding of aggression and violence is undeniable, but the importance of individual characteristics in facilitating violent and aggressive behaviour is of equal importance. The clinician, the clinical psychiatrist, clinical psychologist or clinical criminologist, as West (1980) has emphasized, has an important role in studying offenders as individuals, assessing their peculiarities, and developing programmes which might help them to change their ways, rather than merely to contain or punish them. The clinical approach implies the possibility of treatment, or at least some explanation which can aid prognosis and future management. Although modern radical criminologists find the clinical approach pointless because it appears to ignore the conflicts within society which are responsible for crime, West has powerfully summarized the evidence to justify the continued role of the clinician and the importance of the study of the individual. What we are saying here is that although we may make our contribution to a wider understanding of violent and aggressive behaviour, the expertise of the clinician is primarily concerned with the individual, particularly when his violent behaviour is uncontrolled, uncharacteristic, gratuitous and is possibly related to underlying psychiatric disorder. In practice the clinical expertise of the psychiatrist is required to assist the law in a consideration of criminal responsibility, to evaluate any causal factors and to advise upon or undertake treatment and future management.

The assessment of the individual responsible for a violent act or series of acts must include a consideration of his personality, intelligence, development, family history, relationships (including dynamics of those relationships), and the presence or absence of organic, neurological or toxic factors, together with a presence or absence of mental illness. One is also concerned with the relationship between aggressor and victim and the attempt to reconstruct and understand the circumstances which facilitated violence.

Violent crime is infrequent compared to other types of crime, and the more serious manifestations, such as homicide, are very rare indeed. When looking at the aetiology of the individual, or the circumstances surrounding an act of aggression, there are, unfortunately, only a few rigorous research studies on each type of case. It is necessary to draw evidence from different cultures, comparing the United States with England, for example, which poses obvious problems of interpretation. In the review that follows I have used research studies, single case studies and also clinical experience in order to present as much as possible of the clinical factors involved in aggression. Some of the conclusions are, therefore, based on much more adequate evidence than others, as will be clear to the reader.

Psychopathy

This is not the place to review theories of psychopathy or to repeat the arguments for and against the value of this classification, or allied ones such as sociopathy, character disorder, maladjusted personality and others. Suffice to say that most practising clinicians in this field continue to recognize a group of individuals who stand out from the rest because they exhibit unifying characteristics. Their conduct often brings them into conflict with society; and they appear self-centred and pleasure-seeking, ignoring the restrictions of their particular cultural group. They have failed to learn socialized ways of coping with frustration and anxiety, and they appear unable to establish other than superficial emotional relationships with their fellow men or women. These individuals are highly impulsive, they lack guilt, they fail to learn from experience, and some are abnormally violent and aggressive. Whatever the multifactorial causation of these damaged personalities, they continue to be recognized as a group even though the label that has been applied is now unsatisfactory, because it is so often misunderstood or has been applied so widely. Some individuals are indeed by general standards abnormally aggressive or seriously irresponsible. That we are singularly unsuccessful in devising methods of treatment or management in the medical or sociological field does not mean that we can ignore them or cease to try and understand them. We are particularly concerned here with those in this group who commit violent offences, and who may show an extraordinary lack of concern and disregard for the effect of their behaviour on their victims. Robins (1966), Rutter (1979) and West and Farrington (1977) have carried out detailed longitudinal studies of great importance, which help us to understand the factors which shape not only persistent recidivists but also those who demonstrate personality disorders. In short, the worse the background in terms of deprivation, criminality, disrupted schooling, unstable relationships, broken homes, poverty, family size and many others, the worse the likely outcome.

When it comes to attempting to understand the most aggressive of such individuals what is particularly notable about them is the lack of affection and love which they have received in their own childhood, their lack of control of aggressive impulses, and indifference to the victim as a person rather than an object. Roosenburg (1973), working in Utrecht, describes experiments involving confronting violent criminals with their victims and the positive effect that this had on some of them. Similar experiments have been carried out in the United States. Distancing from the object of aggression and dehumanizing processes which make wartime fighting easier for the ordinary person, appear to be an inherent characteristic among these violent personalities. Another factor which is well known is the experience that such individuals had themselves as children and developing adults, when they were the victims of the violence of their parents or their neglect. As young adults they were often the witnesses of violence, even if they had not already experienced it in childhood. Storr (1978) and Brown and Herrnstein (1974) favour the view that witnessing violence is disinhibitory of violence, making it easier to express rather than provoking it. Another element is that of fear and its projection leading to paranoia: processes easy to understand in the innately insecure individual. In addition one sometimes sees all this developing in an individual in whom the EEG exhibits childhood patterns suggesting delayed maturation of the central nervous system, and in whom there is some indication of early brain damage.

All too rarely does such a person's history, as reported in clinical case records taken during infancy, childhood, and adolescence clearly support this picture, and make it possible to demonstrate that this particular patient differs from others. It is important in these cases, therefore, to obtain as much information as possible by chasing case papers, by interviewing relatives, friends, school teachers and employers, and by scrutinizing criminal records and social work reports. Diagnosis can then be based on established observations during important periods of development and at times of crucial life events rather than relying on the account given by the patient or based upon the hazy recollections of his or her friends.

EEG abnormality and epilepsy

The relationship of EEG abnormality, epilepsy and aggressive behaviour remains an unsatisfactory area. Epilepsy is often considered in cases of sudden impulsive violence and its known presence in an offender may be used by defence lawyers. It is, clear however, that epileptics are not more violent than the general population. Gunn and Fenton (1971) demonstrated some years ago that epileptics are not found in significantly larger numbers among the prison population than elsewhere. A violent attack or even homicide committed during a psychomotor seizure or in a post-ictal state is rare: 36 per cent of 100 children with temporal lobe epilepsy reported by Ounsted (1969) suffered from inter-ictal episodes of rage. The search for temporal lobe abnormalities among those showing severe explosive outbursts of aggression is often fruitless. A number of papers have shown a high incidence of EEG abnormality amongst murderers and others, but in clinical practice this has little significance, and over many years during which an EEG has routinely been carried out in Birmingham it has not been a validated finding. An EEG in the investigation of these cases is only useful when there are clinical indications to suggest epilepsy or organic brain damage. Very rarely, however, cases can be missed and this might justify meticulous investigation. One case was reported by Cope and Donovan (1979) of a man who had repeated prison sentences for violent behaviour and only after some years, and somewhat fortuitously, was found to have a brain tumour. In others a history of head injury with brain damage, perhaps resulting from traffic accidents, has a direct relationship to aggressive outbursts, sometimes leading to the injury of a victim, but again this is a somewhat rare finding.

Alcohol and other toxic agents

Alcohol is the most common toxic agent leading to violence, particularly in Scotland where most homicides are related to alcohol, but there are similar reports in the United States and elsewhere. The general conclusion appears to be that most such episodes are non-premeditated, impulsive and usually involve acquaintances or family members. Many of the victims are also under the influence of alcohol. In some situations alcohol has released underlying paranoid feelings, or longstanding conflict pressures have released controls normally kept well in check. The chronic alcoholic often shows a different pattern and presents as a persistent child or wife beater, his alcoholism often unrecognized until this time even by his wife.

Among other toxic agents, drugs are increasingly prominent, including commonly used medicaments as well as drugs of abuse. Benzodiazepines are widely used tranquillizing drugs which were first thought to have a particularly powerful effect, even on aggressive animals, but it soon became evident that some individuals receiving tranquillizers of this kind demonstrated paradoxical and unexpected aggressive and hostile behaviour. The **British Medical Journal** (Leading article, 18 January 1975) commented that hostile behaviour due apparently to benzodiazepines is something which most clinicians might choose to regard as being so rare as to be of little significance. However, the possibility of such drugs having a disinhibiting effect may have to be borne in mind, for in those patients who are subject to environmental frustration, use of the drug may lead to aggressive or hostile behaviour. This Leader quotes an early case reported by Ingram and Timbury (1960), which concerned a patient taking chlordiazepoxide who physically assaulted his wife for the first time in their 20 years of marraige. It was also noted by my previous colleague, Dr Dennis Morgan in the Department of Psychiatry at Birmingham, that patients undergoing chronic renal haemodialysis who were given diazepam to calm their apprehension often reacted more adversely to the frustrating nature of the procedure than they might otherwise have been expected to do. It is, therefore, worth bearing in mind and taking note of medication received by patients who present with unexpected aggressive or violent behaviour. The patients are also sometimes the victims of drug dependency.

Amphetamines are rarely involved, and their effects are often paradoxical. Ellinwood (1971) has described 13 individuals who committed homicide while intoxicated with amphetamines, but it would seem from a review of the literature that unusually high doses were taken and paranoid psychotic states induced. Some patients present with atypical psychoses associated with cannabis, and a variety of other drugs are sometimes implicated. Paranoid delusions caused by LSD have been documented among a series of homicide cases, and in the United States barbiturates have been described as a responsible toxic agent (see Tinklenberg and Stillman, 1970). More recently the toxic effects of glue sniffing and petrol vapour have been added to the lists of disinhibiting intoxicants.

Psychiatric disorder

The importance of paranoid delusions, particularly delusions of infidelity or morbid jealousy in homicide, have been mentioned widely in the literature and the classic series is that of Mowat from his Broadmoor research in 1966. Such delusions of infidelity are not so uncommon and are sometimes referred to as the Othello Syndrome. The individuals involved are usually of excellent previous character, although sometimes slightly suspicious, but their feelings of hostility, grievance and aggression generally are very powerful. They are, in my opinion, among the most dangerous group in the mentally ill category. They cause wide alarm and they frequently end up in a Special Hospital.

The prevalence of psychiatric disorder amongst violent offenders is not well established, although most clinicians will certainly estimate it as higher than amongst offenders in general. Previous studies of homicidal offenders in England and Wales have shown that about a third demonstrate psychiatric abnormality, and this included mental handicap and psychopathy as well as mental illness. Recent studies have shown a high prevalence of schizophrenia amongst men convicted of homicide and arson (Taylor and Gunn, 1984), and it is probable that schizophrenia is associated with seriously violent behaviour amongst those who have not been under treatment or have been poorly controlled. These authors appear to hint that a possible escalating risk of violence in schizophrenia may be related to current policies of discharging patients with schizophrenia from hospital, or restricting their admission without in many cases providing adequate alternative care.

In England and Wales violence, particularly homicide, is not uncommonly associated with affective disorder, and depressive homicide is one major offence category in which women appear greatly to outnumber men. A substantial proportion of individuals here kill themselves as well as their relatives, but some fail to complete this act and almost always present in a seriously psychotic depressive state requiring urgent treatment. Even then some eventually are so determined that they commit suicide while awaiting trial. I have had several such cases over the years.

In this country family violence has been increasingly studied in connection with child abuse and the parents seem to show recurring characteristics of social deprivation, low frustration tolerance, often low intelligence, a previous experience of violence themselves, and indeed most of the other features described before. In contrast violence by children against parents reveals quite a different picture. Violence directed against fathers is much more common than violence, including matricide, involving mothers. Studying the dynamics of the parent-child relationship prior to the violent outburst is particularly important in these cases. In relation to mothers, clinical experience indicates that there is often an unusually intense mother-child relationship, including a history of severe early maternal restrictiveness with deprivation, provocation and harshness alternating. The father is often uninvolved in the relationship because of his absence or passivity. The violence is often extreme and amnesia is demonstrated afterwards. The act is followed by a sense of relief and self-justification immediately afterwards.

There are more reports of violence against the father, and it has been found that adolescents who make a sudden murderous attack are often rather repressed young men with few social outlets, few sexual outlets, heavily controlled within the family, and are often only children, in whom fear and hatred were evidently being controlled for a considerable period.

During the past 18 months I have had four cases of adolescents killing their parents in isolated country districts where all these features were evident. They all involved shotgun killings of great violence. In every case the young man was a hard-working youth and no outsider had recognized any difficulties within the family. In one case the amnesia described occurred so that no account whatsoever of the murder could be given even up to the time of the trial. Perhaps the most intriguing consideration when one considers the dynamics and tensions within many families is why violence, or even homicide, does not occur in more of them. Many persons share with those who lose control similar character traits and backgrounds ,a lack of tolerance and accumulated excess rage. It is a contellation of factors in dynamic interplay occurring at a particular time involving a unique sequence of events which accounts for the cork being blown at a particular moment in time.

What is the risk of violence among the mentally subnormal? In 1967 the CIBA Foundation held a symposium in London on the subject of the mentally abnormal offender which brought together scholars concerned with this problem from various countries in Europe. One of their principal observations was to comment on the urgent need for more and better empirical data to provide a basis for a reliable assessment. Since then there have been some impressive studies in various parts of the world. These include the important work of Hafner and Boker (1982), who examined the criminal register in West Germany and isolated 533 mentally abnormal offenders representing 3 per cent of all criminals. Offences included homicide, attempted homicide, serious assault and battery. Of these 53 per cent were schizophrenic and 13 per cent mentally retarded, 7 per cent suffered from manic depressive illnesses, 6 per cent from senile dementias, 6 per cent from brain syndromes, 5 per cent from epilepsy and others 10 per cent. From a detailed study of these cases they concluded that the mentally subnormal in general are less likely to commit violent crimes than other people. The 'mentally normal' for this purpose implied no more than an absence of mental illness falling within these categories. There was a slightly higher risk of some specific diagnoses and a slightly lower risk for others, but the diagnostic varation in risk was relatively small. It is necessary, however, to strive to understand the factors that increase risk and make a repetition of a violent act more probable, in order to advise courts, the Parole Board, and the Secretary of State on the likelihood of dangerous behaviour being repeated. Equally, the method of care, management and treatment to be offered to patients, whether or not a secure setting is desirable, depends to a considerable extent on these predictions. What has made the concept of dangerousness even more of an important and live issue is (a) the shortening of the periods of detention which politicians, sentencers and others have justified on various grounds including the increasing pressure on prison space and (b) the reluctance of general psychiatrists to accept the more difficult patient into psychiatric hospitals, the movement towards community care, and the early discharge of patients from hospital.

I have supplied somewhat anecdotally a selection of characteristics which are evident in violent offenders examined after the offence who are diagnosed as suffering from mental disorder. Most mentally abnormal people do not commit violent acts, but I recognize that they are often an unstable and vulnerable group whose predisposition to mental illness has been facilitated by deprived or disadvantaged circumstances, or alternatively they have drifted downwards as a result of coping with an untreated illness. What are the warning signs and the indicators that might suggest an increased risk of violence?

1. A history of criminality and alcoholism particularly in the more severely mentally handicapped is important, and a family history of suicide is relevant for depressives.

2. For the mentally handicapped a background of a broken home with all its consequences is a notable indicator.

3. The presence of anti-social personality traits shown over an extended period of time is an important factor for all categories.

4. A history of overt aggressiveness and particularly a previous history of criminal aggression is generally important, although less significant for depressive offenders.

5. A previous history of attempted suicide is a significant predictor principally in connection with depressives, depressive violence is more likely to be associated with suicide than violence towards others.

6. A history of tense and conflicting relationships with marital or other partners applies particularly to schizophrenics but also to alcoholics, to some extent epileptics, and those with later acquired brain damage and cerebral deterioration. This is probably of little significance for depressives and it does not generally apply to mentally defective offenders who are less often married or involved in intimate partnerships.

7. A history of systematic paranoid delusions, or more rarely delusional jealousy accompanied by the conviction of being harmed, deceived or destroyed by someone is a signal, particularly if the partner in a close, tense, emotional, marital or other intimate relationship is involved in this delusion. This is an observation which is of most relevance in chronic schizophrenics, but also to some extent applies to chronic alcoholics and to those with late acquired brain damage. Delusional fears in depressive patients with an illness of psychotic intensity are similarly important.

8. Increased tension and conflict in social relationships outside the family is relevant in varying degrees to all diagnostic groups.

9. Alcoholism (and alcohol consumption at the time of the crime) is also important.

(derived from Hafner and Boker, 1982)

In the mentally ill the development of uncontrolled illness or deteriorating circumstances is a particularly notable indicator of risk. Equally, absconding from hospital, early discharge, particularly unsatisfactory treatment, or a lack of treatment in the community increases the risk of criminal or violent action.

Prediction

Once a violent act has occurred, we are faced with trying to answer the question, what is the risk of a similar violent act occurring again? The need for more data and more satisfactory research remains crucial. With violent offenders in general our ability to predict the probability of further violence in any particular group is so far very low. We have not yet succeeded in providing criteria which can ensure that a prediction of future violence would be right more often than it would be wrong. If the prediction was more often wrong, and every violent individual was released as soon as he had served whatever sentence the courts thought appropriate, the resulting increase in crimes of violence would be negligible. In fact the great majority of such people are released in relatively short periods of time. However, some are certainly going to repeat their behaviour again, and however inept we are in making predictions we should surely do what we can to try and prevent these acts occurring by attempting to improve our methods of prediction. Perhaps we can say for some that the risk of a further act is negligible (Hamilton and Freeman, 1982). The man of good character who kills his wife during a serious depressive episode is perhaps one such example. We do know and this is one thing on which everyone appears to be agreed, that the best predictor of future violence is a previous conviction for violent crime. The probability increases with each additional known act of violence. When this is repeatedly associated with the much more complex influences of psychotic disorder then we must feel justified in making recommendations for the protection of the offender/patient and others.

A much greater difficulty which follows is the problem of identifying those factors which now reduce the future risk, such as methods of treatment and management. In making these predictions psychiatrists will apply their knowledge of the natural history of the condition, whether it be schizophrenia, depressive psychosis, paranoid state or whatever. They will also be heavily dependent on the contributions of their colleagues, the nurses, the clinical psychologist, and psychotherapist. It is frequently the case that the patient him or herself can tell us nothing about motivation. particularly when the violent behaviour is derived from incomprehensible psychotic processes.

The treatment of mentally abnormal violent offenders is of course primarily the treatment of their mental disorder, but the circumstances and setting in which this treatment takes place, the need for security, and the length of time for which the patient should be detained are important practical considerations. Although this depends to a considerable extent upon the prediction of future violent behaviour, however imprecise and inadequate our prediction techniques might be, the decision on detention is ultimately made by a judge whose responsibility it finally is. Important contributions come from the psychiatrist and his team, and the anonymous group of officials in the Department of Health and Social Security who decide whether or not a person should be admitted to a Special Hospital. The availability of resources is also important. Whatever predictions we may make, the horror and enormity of the behaviour, the perceived public reaction and past record will play equally important or greater parts in forming the final decision. resources. Whatever predictions we may make, the horror and enormity of the behaviour, the perceived public reaction and past record will play equally important or greater parts in forming the final decision.

This whole area has been very unsatisfactory for a considerable time, and particularly since the advent of open-door hospitals and a rejection of difficult patients. The increasing intolerance of violence in hospitals, even for quite minor aggressive behaviour, has highlighted this problem. The danger is not of course insignificant and there have been increasing reports and studies on the prevalence of violent behaviour towards nursing staff and other patients over the years. The Confederation of Health Service Employees 1977 Report noted with increasing alarm the steadily rising numbers of violent assaults by patients upon psychiatric nursing staff and have produced guidelines on the management of such patients in the Health Service. The Report of the Committee on Mentally Abnormal Offenders (The Butler Report) had already addressed this problem in its Reports (e.g. 1975). This has led to the development of the Regional Secure Unit programme, the emergence of which complements the more careful selection on the one hand and the movement to community care on the other. Our aim here is to move towards the provision of a range of specialized facilities for the care of patients who are thought to provide a risk, from maximum security at one end of the scale, to the provision of various levels of security in the middle, and to a greater tolerance in open facilities at the other end. We are now making some progress and I have recently described the development of the Secure Unit programme (Bluglass, 1985) in a volume which examines the whole issue of secure accommodation.

A great deal of money has been spent by successive governments in providing these new facilities, which will provide new opportunities for research into phenomonology, diagnosis, treatment and prediction. It is important that all of us from whatever profession collaborate and take advantage of the opportunities that we are given to make new inroads into an understanding of this subject. Equally we should all ensure that having established new services we do not in the future become the poor relations not just of the Health Service but of the psychiatric service, and that the secure units do not replace the Victorian mental hospitals as the new problem areas of the 21st century as a result of lack of funding and support. Equally, support, follow-up and community services are essential to reduce the risk of violent behaviour after discharge. It is essential that such support is established and that we have created a caring community before over-enthusiastically insisting upon too early discharge to community care.

References

BLUGLASS, R. (1985) The development of regional secure units. In: L. Gostin (ed.) **Secure Provision.** London: Tavistock

BRITISH MEDICAL JOURNAL (1975) Leading article. **British Medical Journal, 256**

BROWN, R. and HERRNSTEIN, R. (1974) **Psychology.** London: Methuen

BUTLER COMMITTEE (1975) **Report on the Committee of Mentally Disordered Offences.** Cmnd 6244. London: HMSO.

CONFEDERATION OF HEALTH SERVICE EMPLOYEES (1977) **The Management of Violent or Potentially Violent Patients.** London: COHSE

COPE, R. and DONOVAN, M. (1979) A case of insane automatism? **British Journal of Psychiatry, 135,** 574-575

ELLINWOOD, E. (1971) Assault and homicide associated with amphetamine abuse. **American Journal of Psychiatry, 127,** 1170-1175

GUNN, J. and FENTON, G. (1971) Epilepsy, automatism and crime. **Lancet, 1,** 1173-1176

HAFNER, H. and BOKER, W. (1982) **Crimes of Violence by Mentally Abnomal Offenders.** Cambridge: Cambridge University Press

HAMILTON, J. and FREEMAN, H. (1982) **Dangerousness: Assessment and management.** London: Gaskell Press

INGRAM, I.M. and TIMBURY, G. (1960) Side effects of librium. **Lancet, 2,** 766

MOWAT, R.R. (1966) **Morbid Jealousy and Murder.** London: Tavistock

OUNSTED, C. (1969) Aggression and epilepsy: rage in children with temporal lobe epilepsy. **Journal of Psychosomatic Research, 13,** 237-242

ROBINS, L. (1966) **Deviant Children Grown Up.** Baltimore: Williams & Wilkins

ROOSENBURG, A.M. (1973) Resozialisierung in der van der Hoevenkliniek. **Pro Infirmis,** 8-16

RUTTER, M. (1979) **Changing Youth in a Changing Society.** London: Nuffield Provincial Hospitals Trust

STORR, A. (1968) **Human Aggression.** London: Allen Lane

STORR, A. (1978) Sadism and paranoia: cruelty as collective and individual response. In: L.A. Hersov, M. Berger and D.D. Shaffer (eds) **Aggression and Antisocial Behaviour in Childhood and Adolescence.** Oxford: Pergamon Press

TAYLOR, P.J. and GUNN, J. (1984) Violence and psychosis. **British Medical Journal, 288,** 1945-1949

TINKLENBERG, J.R. and STILLMAN, R.C. (1970) Drug use and violence. In: D.N. Daniels, M.F. Gilula, and F.M. Ochberg (eds) **Violence and the Struggle for Existence.** Boston: Little, Brown & Co

WEST, D.J. and FARRINGTON, D.P. (1977) **The Delinquent Way of Life.** London: Heinemann Educational Books

WEST, D.J. (1980) The clinical approach to criminology. **Psychological Medicine, 10,** 619-631

THE PHYSICAL ABUSE OF CHILDREN

Neil Frude

For an audience of this nature I hardly need to spell out the basic facts about the physical abuse of children. A number of children die each year at the hands of their parents or care-givers - the figure is in the region of 100 per year - but this represents only the tip of a very large iceberg. Precise figures for 'lower level' abuse are difficult to obtain for a number of reasons, and of course it depends how we define physical abuse and what criterion level we apply.

By now a great deal of research has been done on the subject. Much is known about the psychological effects of abuse and the characteristics of the abusing parent. A number of approaches to risk identification, treatment and prevention have been developed. I will be presenting a simple model of child abuse and then discussing some of the ways in which the model can be used to suggest strategies for treatment. I will not be too concerned in this paper in citing the numerous research studies which underlie my argument, but I will later quote a few sources where full references and other details may be obtained.

In this context I am going to concentrate on the psychology of the 'perpetrator' or 'aggressor'. A full picture of the 'psychology of abuse' would of course include a review of the psychological effects on the child. It is also important to consider the interactions between parent and child and the nature of the relationship between them. But here I am going to focus on the parent and ask the simple question: 'Why do parents sometimes physically attack and harm their children?'.

This is slightly different from the question 'What sort of parent hurts a child?'. Numerous research studies have been conducted in an attempt to identify the characteristics of the abusing parent. Taking, say, 50 parents who are known to have abused their children and comparing them with 50 parents who have not, it has been possible to identify various statistical differences between the two populations. We know that the abusing parents tend to be young, working class, with 'difficult' babies or young children. We know that they tend to be under stress, living in relatively impoverished surroundings and isolated from the community. We also know that they themselves are likely to have been victims of physical abuse.

Altogether over 500 variables have been identified as differentiating statistically between the groups. However, on any of these variables there is some degree of overlap between the groups. On social class, for example, most working-class parents do not abuse their children and some middle-class parents do. There is in fact no criterion variable or combination of variables which can enable us to identify accurately the abusing parent, though certain characteristics may be associated with an increased risk of abuse. Such correlates of abuse are of limited clinical relevance for they are limited in their predictive power. Second, many of them are not easily susceptible to change (social class, for example, or the age of the parent, or the parent's personality). Third, such correlates may not provide clues about the cause of abuse. Finally, with 500 or so correlates we have an embarrassingly rich data base, one which would seem unlikely to provide a comprehensible conceptual model.

There is another important point. The abusive act is a particular event rather than a constant 'on-going situation'. Parental behaviour which actually results in injury to a child is likely to occur only once or twice during childhood. Thus the 'stable characteristics' (like social class and social isolation) are unlikely to provide an adequate explanation of why, on a particular day at a particular time, the parent beat the child so severely that serious injury resulted. For a more adequate explanation, therefore, the time-scale needs to be contracted. We need, perhaps, to integrate the background variables into a model which, nevertheless, focuses on the abuse incident. It may be useful to understand many aspects of the abusing parent's personality, and of the relationship between child and parent but, ultimately, we want to know why that parent behaved in such a way at that particular time that the result was a fractured skull or an abdominal haemorrhage. Whatever else physical abuse is, it is an act of aggression. We have a good 'common-sense' understanding of aggression based on our extensive experience as 'social beings' and, in addition, psychologists have built up over the years a more specialist vocabulary, more refined conceptualizations, and a considerable array of facts concerning aggression. Before generating a specific set of models to explain child abuse, therefore, it would be wise to examine the more general models to see whether or not child abuse can be understood within such a framework.

Some years ago I attempted to do this and, as far as I was concerned, child abuse could indeed be understood as a particular example of aggression (Frude, 1980). My approach was to collect together the many facts concerning abuse and to see whether they could be successfully matched with a general model of aggression. I was, of course, wishing to focus principally on the abuse incident. In addition, I wanted a scheme that would be flexible enough to be able to deal with the many different forms that physical child abuse can take. Even the most casual glance at case histories will convince the reader that not all cases are the same. There is, indeed, a prodigious heterogeneity between cases.

A model for aggression

The simple model I took conceptualized the aggressive incident in the following manner:

SITUATION → APPRAISAL → ANGER → INHIBITION → AGGRESSION

SITUATION
First, there is usually, although not always, some objective situation which triggers aggression. An observer can usually see why somebody has become aggressive and the aggressor, in later reports, will almost always give some external event as at least contributing to his or her aggression.

APPRAISAL

Most external situational events can be interpreted in a number of ways, a charitable interpretation may attenuate any emotional response. How we judge the situation clearly influences our reaction. 'Appraisal styles' are likely to differ from person to person, and from time to time.

ANGER

An event may be judged in such a way that we become angry. Our underlying mood, or previous events, may have set our emotional tone so that the identical 'appraised event' will have quite differeces emotional consequences at different times. Again, some people may be more likely to become angry than others. There are likely to be individual differences in 'threshold for anger', with some people being very placid and others more emotionally reactive.

INHIBITION/FACILITATION

Not all anger leads to an aggressive act. Even where the level of anger is considerable, internal inhibitions and social inhibitions may lead the individual to 'bottle it up'. On the other hand, internal or external 'goading' may reduce the inhibitions, facilitating the expression of the anger as open aggression.

AGGRESSION

Clearly this may take many forms. Verbal abuse, shouting and table-thumping are examples of the non-dangerous 'safe' expression of anger. Slapping, punching and kicking are dangerous forms. The precise nature of the physical attack, the position that blows land on the victim's body, and the physical vulnerability of the victim, all influence the damage which will result.

This scheme for describing 'stages' in the aggressive incident will form the framework for the rest of what I have to say. Some points need to be made to clarify the schema. The additional 'loop' is included to encompass the fact that not all aggression is powered by anger. Sometimes aggression is 'instrumental', that is, motivated not by anger but by the desire to achieve some positive outcome from the act of aggression. Thus the aggression of the 'mugger' is instrumental. The mugger is not angry with the victim but uses aggression more 'coldly' to obtain the contents of a handbag. There have been reported cases of instrumental aggression in child abuse but they are exceedingly rare. Generally, it is the anger-aggression pathway which best describes the nature of abusive incidents.

Another point is that there are many 'feedback loops' from one element in the scheme to another. Thus anger may influence appraisal (i.e. how an event is judged) and an aggressive outburst is likely to generate a response which is yet another event which will be appraised and responded to emotionally and behaviourally. Before turning to see how physical abuse may be fitted into this schema, let me provide some simple examples of more general aggression to illustrate the model. The situation which triggers aggression is usually social. We all know how we might attempt to trigger aggression in somebody. We could insult them, criticize them harshly, make faces at them, or step on their toe. Now, placing ourselves in the victim's position, we can see how appraisal works. If someone comes up to me and steps on my toe I can interpret this charitably as an accident (in which case I probably wouldn't become angry) or as a vicious gesture (in which case I would). If a stranger made a face at me I might judge him in terms of some psychiatric diagnostic class and ignore it, or I might judge him to be in full possession of his senses and get very angry.

If I'm angry with someone I do try not to become openly aggressive as I have healthy internal inhibitions, but sometimes they're not sufficient. Then my control depends largely on where I am, who's watching and what the likely consequences of aggression might be. The fear of physical or legal retaliation might well lead me to sit on my anger. If I've been angered and the same person then steps on my toe again this might prove too much. For one thing, I'm unlikely to appraise the second toe-tread as accidental. For another, that might just be the last straw and push my anger past the level at which I can hold it in. Notice, then, how sequences of events may change the appraisal tendencies and how anger may accumulate.

In some cases a situation is such that anybody would be angered. The viciousness of the 'other' is so obvious that it would be appraised negatively even by the proverbial saint. In other cases, however, the situation would be seen by the majority as relatively benign. Only those with rather strange ideas would take offence. Some people may be of such a temperament that they are constantly casting about for any event that can be construed as an 'offence' against them. So already we are building in a degree of flexibility to the model. Some acts of aggression stem from truly unbearable situations, others from bizarre styles of judgement. In the majority of cases, perhaps, both the objective situation and the style of judgement need to be considered in order to understand the anger which results. Clearly there will be major differences in the 'ambient level' of anger, different thresholds and different levels of 'emotional amplification' in response to the appraised event.

There are also major individual differences in inhibitions. Some people who are often angry nevertheless have high levels of behavioural control. Others have an abiding fear of the external consequences of aggression. And, finally, while some people habitually shout when angry, others hit out. Some stamp their feet while others are ever 'ready with their fists'. The influences which affect the various stages along that pathway are many. There are likely to be sex differences (in appraisal? in anger levels? in inhibitions? in habitual patterns of aggressive behaviour?); perhaps there are age differences, too. Individual differences in, say, appraisal style or inhibitions, may reflect social class or aspects of home background. Anger thresholds may be affected by stress, hormonal changes associated with the menstrual cycle, alcohol use, etc. Thus we can see how this approach may incorporate the many longer-term correlates which have been found for child abuse, while also accommodating the many ways in which cases may differ one from the other.

One last point before I focus exclusively on child abuse. The model is progressive. Generally, at least, there is a situational trigger. This is not sufficient to cause aggression, however. It must be appraised. There must then be anger. There must then be a lack of inhibition. Intervention, therefore, can focus on a number of points. We might change the situation. This in itself, if successful, would prevent the aggression. Or, without affecting the situation, we might attempt to modify the appraisal so that it was always charitable. Or, at the later stage, we could teach anger control methods directly affecting the emotional response or, by increasing inhibitions, we might prevent the anger from being behaviourally expressed. Finally we could address ourselves to the aggression itself, perhaps changing the habitual punch to a verbal outburst, or at least changing a dangerous punch to a vulnerable part of the body into a relatively harmless slap to a non-vulnerable part.

Thus our model provides us with numerous alternative strategies for intervention and the possibility, of course, for simultaneous attention to several different points of focus along the pathway. In other contexts I have applied this general model usefully to the fields of marital violence, sex differences in aggression, and the effects of alcohol on aggression. I make no claim to originating the model. Indeed, one of its strengths is how closely it tallies with our naive understanding of the nature of aggressive acts. I've also been able to show that the same model was implicit in the anger theory of Seneca, the ancient Roman philosopher, and that it is implicit in children's understanding of aggression from the age of five years. I now want to apply this very simple and general model to the specific field of child abuse. I'll first trace through the stages and show how the model can be used to integrate various research findings and case studies.

Applying the model to child abuse

SITUATION
In almost all cases of child abuse the attack is triggered by some action of the child. Parents do not attack the passive, sleeping child. Typically the trigger is prolonged crying or screaming in the case of babies, or, for older children, some act of defiance or 'naughtiness'. In Scott's (1973) study of 29 male prisoners who had fatally injured their children each case was said to have been precipitated by some special behaviour of the child. A number of research reports testify to the role of the screaming baby in triggering abuse. Terr (1970) quoted examples in which an attack had apparently been precipitated by extreme acts of naughtiness (including an incident in which clothes were cut to pieces, and one in which a child defaecated into a laundry basket full of clean clothes).

In a survey I conducted in Cardiff with Alison Goss, (1980) serious attacks w always associated with some environmental trigger. One child had powdered a new carpet with scouring powder, another had painted with nail varnish over a new bedroom suite. Countless episodes of screaming and prolonged crying triggered aggression. Abused children, compared with their non-abused peers, tend to be 'naughty', they are more likely to have behaviour disorders, and they are more likely to be congenitally handicapped. There is also some evidence that they may be less attractive and that, as babies, they tend to scream in a particularly unpleasant way.

APPRAISAL
At a purely sensory level, some parents are more sensitive to screaming than others. One abusive mother told the NSPCC (1976) 'I can't stand to hear a child scream, it goes right through me'. Others feel physically nauseous when they see a child eating messily, and their revulsion soon turns to anger when they judge that the child is being careless in his or her eating. Dangerous, anger-provoking appraisals often stem from one of two factors: a 'negative set' with regard to the particular child, or unduly high expectations of children's behaviour, based on an unrealistic appreciation of child psychology. An NSPCC research report (1976) indicated that abusing mothers frequently misconstrue their children's moods and may attribute evil intentions to the child even at the baby stage. Thus one mother, disturbed by her baby's crying during her favourite soap opera, felt that the child was 'deliberately' interrupting the programme. Brandon (1976) quotes an example where a baby's 'look' was inappropriately interpreted: 'He looks at me as if to say "Just you try and feed me".'

Steele and Pollock (1968) quote a case in which a mother said: 'When he cried all the time, it meant he didn't love me, so I hit him'. Sometimes parents have totally unrealistic notions about how clean or tidy or obedient children generally are and judge their own child's 'normal' behaviour as exceptional and blameworthy. Research shows that abusing parents tend to have extremely high expectations of their children and have little appreciation of the true 'norms' of behaviour.

ANGER

Prior to the abuse incident the parent is often in a highly aroused state. Anger may have accumulated during a difficult day. An example of this is found in Steele and Pollock's (1968) case of 'Larry'. He lost his job one day and when he went home and reported this to his wife she walked out on him, leaving him alone with the baby. When the baby started to cry Larry was unable to find the feeding bottle. Looking everywhere, with the hungry baby crying louder and louder, totally frustrated and unable to satisfy the hunger, Larry's temper finally exploded and he beat the child severely. Abuse incidents are also associated with situations in which the anger threshold is noticeably lowered. Thus in situations of extreme marital tension, of pre-menstrual stress, and of extreme tiredness, abuse appears to be more likely.

INHIBITION

Most people seem to have fairly high levels of inhibition against hitting a child dangerously, but this may be overcome in situations of extreme anger. Some abuse may result from such extreme situations, but some abusing parents do have rather low levels of inhibition. Abusing parents do have a general tendency to use physical means of punishment. They often believe that it is a parent's right and duty to discipline the child strictly and they may fear that, without strong discipline, the child may 'run amok' or become 'spoilt'. They therefore justify their habitual use of smacking.

Whereas those who are more restrained about physical discipline generally may escalate their behaviour to a smack in times of great provocation, those who use a smack habitually may in such exceptional circumstances escalate to more serious and dangerous forms of attack. Inhibitions about particular forms of aggression may lessen with experience: 'The first time I hit her it was only a small blow and I cried all the rest of the day. I swore to myself I'd never lift a finger to her again. But it was only a few days after when she drove me mad with her crying and I hit her even harder. It sort of escalated, I hit her a bit harder each time' (Renvoize, 1978). On the other hand, inhibitions may be strengthened as the result of a shocking experience: 'I was going out and she was getting in the way. Then I picked her up and I just threw her. She banged her head on the side of the wall. I was so frightened. I felt so sorry for her. Never again'. (Frude and Goss, 1980).

AGGRESSION

The precise form of aggression used is very important, it may be a matter of life and death. Several factors seem to influence which form of aggression is used. One of these is <u>habits.</u> It seems that parents develop general habits with regard to the method of discipline and that these are often merely exaggerated in extreme circumstances. Those who habitually use verbal forms may escalate to more extreme verbal forms. Those who slap may slap more harshly. Those who use a stick for the more ritual disciplining may use this later as a deadly weapon. There is some suggestion (Gelles, 1973) that a parent will often use as the preferred means of discipline the method which was used to control them in childhood.

INSTRUMENTAL ACTION

Even when aggression stems from anger, the precise action used might have an apparent instrumental purpose. Thus a pillow may be held against the face of a screaming child. One mother reported (NSPCC, 1976) 'I put my hand over his mouth to shut him up and suddenly I realized that he'd stopped breathing and was quite limp'. A child who won't eat may be force-fed, a spoon being used as a feeding instrument cum weapon, producing broken teeth and bleeding gums.

THREAT EXECUTION

Verbal threats, even of a bizarre variety, may be used as warnings of dire punishments, and sometimes these threats may be acted upon literally in extreme circumstances. Thus a mother who had threatened to throw her child into a hot oven, presumably meaning this initially as an empty threat, did just this when extremely provoked (Renvoize, 1974).

SYMBOLIC ACTION

Some actions seem to have a symbolic content. Young (1964) reported a case in which pepper was rubbed into the genitals of a little girl who had been 'touching herself'. This is an appropriate point at which to raise the issue of 'displacement'. Sometimes the victim of an attack attracts far more aggression than is 'due' to him. Anger elicited by another person is directed towards the child. Seldom will the child have been passive, but the aggression may be disproportionate to any perceived offence. Thus one mother reported: 'He's the absolute image of his father which is why I think he comes in for, you know, a lot of punishment. I look at him and see Clive' (Renvoize, 1974).

Finally, in this section, I'll say just a word about the far rarer types of child abuse. First, some illustrations of instrumental child abuse. Skinner and Castle (1969) quote the case in which a mother and father seemed to deliberately injure their child, believing that they would thereby gain more 'points' in the competition for council accommodation. Luckianowicz (1971) quotes a case in which an unwanted child was beaten. The mother then presented herself to her GP as an 'abusing parent' in order that the child be removed from her care. There are also the rare cases in which abuse stems from sadistic tendencies or psychotic states. In one reported case a father seemed to gain pleasure from hurting his daughter and pulled out her fingernails, one a day, for ten days. In another case a schizophrenic mother believed that her son was the incarnation of the devil and ritually slayed him. It cannot be emphasized enough that such cases are extremely rare. In the vast majority of cases the abusive incident can be best understood in terms of the general anger-induced aggression model.

Treatment: general points

We now come to the implications of this model for clinical intervention in child abuse cases. Some general points can be made:

1. There are obviously many possible target areas along the pathway: we may change the situation, the appraisal, the anger, the level of inhibitions or the nature of the aggressive act.

2. Change at any one of these levels may have the desired effect of preventing the harmful expression of anger injuring the child.

3. More than one element along the pathway may be subject to intervention at any one time.

4. Treatment modes may be focused directly on an element or on some factor which influences an element (for example, the parent-child relationship, pre-menstrual tension, the marital relationship).

5. The point(s) for intervention should reflect the individual nature of the case. Thus where the situation is truly unbearable it may be the most appropriate element for change. Where the appraisal style contributes much to the anger it may be a special treatment target and so forth.

Treatment specifics

I will concentrate on those forms of intervention which focus directly on the pathway I have been describing. It is not difficult to apply many standard forms of treatment to the various elements. This may be done in a formal treatment setting, by highly trained personnel such as clinical psychologists, or may be less formal. Several interventions, indeed, may be handed on to the client as a 'tip' for dealing with unbearable situational provocation or in times of special emotional need. There is also considerable evidence, from our own study in Cardiff, that non-abusing parents successfully use various strategies to control their aggression in the face of difficult child behaviour. As we shall see later, many of these bear an uncanny resemblance to the more formal treatment methods.

Parents will often admit that they have difficulty in controlling their temper with a child. Some contact 'parent help lines' for advice, others confide in a health visitor or GP. In some cases there will be a history of abuse, with the parents seeking professional help to prevent recurrence. Clearly it is much easier to pass on tips or start a treatment programme if the parent admits to the danger, but it may be better in many cases to characterize the situation as one in which help is being given for parenting difficulties rather than stressing the danger of physical damage.

The first stage would be to attempt to understand the individual case in the terms I have described. Talking with the parent or parents and observing the child will identify the extent to which the child's behaviour is itself a real problem - the extent to which the 'situation' is especially difficult. Next comes some assessment of the extent to which 'appraisal' presents a special problem. What acts of the child irritate the parents? Do they have realistic expectations of a child of that age and ability level? Are their standards too high? Do they seem to have a 'down' on the child, leading them to appraise the child's actions negatively?

Next we would want to ask them about their anger levels. Are there patterns to their anger feelings? Do they let anger build up over time? Do they have ways of controlling their anger? On the question of inhibitions we need to know whether they seek to justify their attacks? What do they believe to be a reasonable level of discipline? Finally, how do they chastise the child? Do they use instruments, do they punch? Do they realize the danger of shaking a child?

In this way it is possible to build a profile of the case and to identify particular sources of danger. This is likely to point to one or more suitable targets for intervention.

SITUATION

If the situation is abnormal it may be possible to change it. The child's behaviour may itself be a target for change. Hyperactivity, excessive crying, bed-wetting and soiling may be modified by behavioural methods. It is possible that a change in sleeping arrangements or increased sharing of parental responsibilities may reduce the incidence of some of the difficulties.

APPRAISAL

If a high sensitivity to screaming seems to be the fundamental problem then it might be possible to arrange for a formal desensitization programme, in which the client is relaxed while listening to tapes of progressively more obnoxious screams. There are successful reports of such interventions in the literature, although simpler alternative strategies might be preferred (such as instructing the parent to leave the room when the child is screaming). If the parents have a bizarre notion of child 'norms' this may be changed by counselling. Parents may need to learn that babies do not cry 'intentionally' and that soiling is not 'deliberate'. Someone whom they respect as more 'expert' than they are may be able to convince them that the child's behaviour does not in fact have the machiavellian or evil 'meaning' which they attribute to it.

If they have a special 'down' on the child then the focus of treatment would be the child-parent relationship. What can be done to increase the parent's affection for and esteem of the child? It is possible to teach alternative appraisal styles so that parents are encouraged to 'make excuses for the child', to 'think of the good times' or to attribute screaming to 'teething'. An appraisal of 'naughtiness' as deliberate malevolence and viciousness may be changed so that it becomes mere 'mischief'. It may be news to the parents that 'all children are naughty sometimes' and they may consequently change their perception so that the child is seen as 'normal' rather than 'delinquent'.

ANGER

There are several well-tested methods for controlling anger. Relaxation is one, counting to ten another. Several traditional methods have now been incorporated into cognitive-behaviour therapy. Thus parents may be encouraged to use such 'self-statements' as: 'Just breathe slowly, stay calm, and relax for a minute'. Such methods have been evaluated in a wide variety of anger-eliciting contexts including those of potential child abuse (Doctor and Singer, 1978).

INHIBITIONS
These may be increased in a variety of ways. One of the most obvious is to threaten the parents with the legal consequences of abuse. Another strategy involves explaining to the parents the potential physical and psychological dangers of abusive actions. Thus parents may feel that shaking the child is 'safe' since it leaves no obvious mark. A warning that severe shaking might lead to brain damage may be sufficient to raise their inhibitions about this particular action. Parents who feel themselves to be on the threshold of attacking the child and who are 'at the end of their tether' may be encouraged to take the child outside the home into a public place where the social situation may act as an effective inhibitor. Those with a telephone may be encouraged to contact a relative or professional during times of particular stress, either to talk about their immediate problem or merely to make contact with another adult. Thus the presence or telephone presence of a friend or stranger will usually have the desirable effects of calming the individual and providing a social 'witness' to inhibit extreme action.

AGGRESSION
It may be possible to change the parents' habitual disciplining behaviour. Indicating that there is a sharp line to be drawn between 'acceptable' or 'non-dangerous' discipline and that which is likely to be truly abusive, may lead the parents to modify their actions. Detailing punishments which are alternatives to physical discipline may come as a revelation. Sending the older child to bed or depriving him or her of privileges may ultimately prove effective for control, and is certainly less dangerous. Parents may be convinced by such an argument. I don't have space to detail such strategies as I have briefly described. Details of the more formal treatment modes can be found in many sources. A useful compendium, specifically concerned with child abuse, is provided by Kelly (1983). Kelly emphasizes the need to tailor the treatment to the specific characteristics of the individual case, and his approach fits in well with the model I have described. His book includes full details on the clinical assessment of child-abusive families and provides such 'tools' as relaxation scripts and scenarios for training parents to use 'time out' and other behavioural strategies as an alternative to violent forms of discipline.

Self-control in non-abusive mothers

I claimed earlier that many parents use strategies to control their aggressive behaviour towards the child and that many of these shadow the effective intervention techniques. In this final phase of my paper I will share with you some of the methods reported by the real 'experts' in abuse prevention, those parents who find themselves in thoroughly provoking situations and yet do <u>not</u> become abusive. A few years ago Alison Goss and I conducted a survey on 100 mothers in South Wales (Frude and Goss, 1980). Each had a child between four and six years of age. We asked them about their difficulties with the child and how they had coped in the four years or so since the birth of that child.

Many reported difficult situations and half said that they felt that at times they could have injured the child. We asked them to tell us how they coped in such circumstances and they provided a rich array of self-control strategies. You'll hardly be surprised to learn that both their accounts of particular incidents and their strategies for self-control fit well into the model I have described. In view of the limited time I'll describe only the latter. Details of the study have been published in Frude (1980).

SITUATION
Some mothers who felt themselves being provoked by the child would leave the room. Others would disengage themselves from the child's irritating behaviour by simply doing something which distracted them.

APPRAISAL
Some used specific formulae to set their mind in such a way that they viewed the child's behaviour sympathetically. One mother would tell herself that 'children know no better' and another said she concentrated hard on how small and dependent the child was. One of our subjects would block out the annoyed appraisal by recalling scenes from a happy holiday, while another called to mind 'scriptural references on family life'.

ANGER
Some strategies seemed aimed at 'dissolving' anger while others focused on actively 'discharging' it. The 'discharging' behaviours included foot-stamping, screaming, 'screaming inside' and bursting into tears. Several of the 'anger dissolving strategies' involved various accepted methods of self-calming and relaxing. Deep breathing and 'counting to ten' were frequently used. Some mothers lit a cigarette to 'calm their nerves' and one took a tranquillizer. One would put on a record of soothing music, one splashed her face with cold water and another used 'level B of the relaxation I learned for the birth of my babies'.

INHIBITION
One woman increased her inhibition about aggression by concentrating on the remorse which she knew she would feel later if she hit the child. Others mentioned the fear that a relative might see a bruise.

Conclusion

In cases where parents admit that they have problems in dealing with their child, problems that they feel might lead to physical abuse or extreme anger, there are many ways in which a professional might intervene. So many parents find themselves regularly in highly provocative situations with their child that we might, indeed, wonder that there is so little abuse. The reason seems to be that many parents have developed effective means of control. They have much to tell us - much that they and we may 'pass on' to parents with difficulties.

The principal value of a model such as the one I have described is not that it integrates much of the rather varied knowledge concerning the characteristics of abusive populations, or even that it immediately suggests treatment strategies. The principal value is that it conveys the idea that abuse may be seen as an unfortunate extreme of the 'normal' parenting situation rather than as odd, unfathomable behaviour perpetrated by weird and unfathomable people. The model thus presents a perspective which at once demystifies abuse, relating it directly to experiences which are common to us all, and identifies it as a problem likely to be amenable to a solution via rational treatment.

References

BRANDON, S. (1976) Physical violence in the family: an overview. In: M. Borland (ed.) **Violence in the Family.** Manchester: Manchester University Press

DOCTOR, R.M. and SINGER, E.M. (1978) Behavioural intervention strategies with child abusive parents. **Child Abuse and Neglect, 2,** 57-68

FRUDE, N.J. (1980) Child abuse as aggression. In: N.J. Frude (ed.) **Psychological Approaches to Child Abuse.** London: Batsford Academic

FRUDE, N.J. and GOSS, A. (1980) Maternal anger and the young child. In: N.J. Frude (ed.) **Psychological Approaches to Child Abuse.** London: Batsford Academic

GELLES, R.J. (1973) Child abuse as psychopathology: a sociological critique and reformulation. **American Journal of Orthopsychiatry, 43,** 611-621

KELLY, J. (1983) **Treating Child Abusive Families: Intervention based on skills training principles.** New York: Plenum

LUCKIANOWICZ, N. (1971) Battered children. **Psychiatrica Clinica, 4,** 257-280

NSPCC (1976) **At Risk: An account of the work of the battered child research department, NSPCC.** London: Routledge & Kegan Paul

RENVOIZE, J. (1974) **Children in Danger.** London: Routledge & Kegan Paul

RENVOIZE, J. (1978) **Violence in the Family.** London: Routledge & Kegan Paul

SCOTT, P. (1973) Parents who kill their children. **Medicine, Science and Law, 13,** 120-126

SKINNER, A.E., and CASTLE, R.L. (1969). **78 Battered Children: A retrospective study.** London: NSPCC

STEELE, B.F. and POLLOCK, C.B. (1968) A psychiatric study of parents who abuse infants and small children. In: R.E. Helfer and C.H. Kempe (eds) **The Battered Child.** Chicago: University of Chicago Press

TERR, L.C. (1970) A family study of child abuse. **American Journal of Psychiatry, 127,** 665-671

YOUNG, L. (1964) **Wednesday's Children.** New York: McGraw Hill

BEHAVIOUR MODIFICATION OF CHILDREN WITH AGGRESSIVE CONDUCT DISORDERS: THE USE OF TRIADIC MODEL INTERVENTIONS IN HOME SETTINGS

Martin Herbert

Introduction

It is very difficult to select what to include in a relatively brief paper from about 12 or more years' work with aggressive (conduct-disordered) children in their natural environments - mainly 'own home' or residential care settings. Natural environment interventions, in contrast to clinic-based treatment, seek to utilize the ongoing and intensive influence of those in close, everyday contact with the client in attempting to modify deviant behaviour and teach new skills and behavioural repertoires. The triadic model, as it is called, by-passes the problem of generalizing improvements from the consulting room to the outside world. Parents and teachers - as primary mediators of change - are 'in situ' most of the time, and are in a position to apply contingencies in a variety of situations.

This paper presents a few comments on the practical aspects of our work at the Child Treatment Research Unit (CTRU) based at the Psychology Department in the University of Leicester. Further details of the approach and its efficacy are published in Herbert (1981, 1985). We have tried to work at both the remedial and preventive aspects of aggressive and other disorders in children.

Prognosis

It is difficult to provide a base rate for aggressive conduct problems because of difficulties of definition and a paucity of longitudinal evidence. But unlike the development of fears and many other problems of childhood, there is not the same tendency for the conduct problems to be transitory. Early aggression - when intense and high in frequency - must be taken seriously. Writers like Robins (1966) suggest that by age 7 or 8 the child with <u>extreme</u> antisocial aggresssive patterns of behaviour is at quite considerable risk of continuing on into adolescence and indeed adulthood with serious deviancy of one kind or another. Lefkowitz et al. (1977) followed a group of New York children from age 8 to age 19 years; their study has a particular focus on the persistence of aggression. Aggression was much less common in girls than in boys but in both sexes children who were highly aggressive at age 8 tended also to be unduly aggressive at 19 years (correlations of 0.38 for boys and 0.47 for girls). In West and Farrington's study of London boys substantial continuity was again shown (Farrington, 1979). Of the youths rated most aggressive at 8 to 10 years, 59 per cent were in the most aggressive group at 12 to 14 years (compared with 29 per cent of the remaining boys) and 40 per cent were so at 16 to 18 years (compared with 27 per cent of the remainder). The boys who were severely aggressive at 8 to 10 years were especially likely to become violent delinquents (14 per cent versus 4.5 per cent).

The same study demonstrated the very considerable extent to which troublesome, difficult and aggressive behaviour in young boys was associated with later juvenile delinquency. Both the measure at age 8 to 10 years of 'combined conduct disorder', which was based on combined ratings of teachers and social workers, and that of 'troublesomeness' at the same age, which was a combined rating of peers and teachers, proved to be powerful predictors of delinquency. This was especially so with respect to severe and persistent delinquency going on into adult life. Some half of such individuals showed deviant ratings on these measures compared with only one in six of non-delinquent boys.

For our present purposes, aggressive behaviour refers to socially unacceptable ways of behaving which may result in physical or psychological injury to another person or in damage to property. The social learning approach (the one adopted here) treats aggression as a complex event which requires an explanation of behaviour that produces injurious and destructive effects as well as social labelling processes (i.e. the social judgements that decide which acts are labelled 'aggressive').

Social learning approach: previous learning experience

There is a somewhat surprising consensus - and a confidently expressed one - that aggressive behaviour in children can be related to long-term attitudes and child-rearing practices. To summarize the findings, parental permissiveness of aggression is said to increase the child's tendency to behave aggressively (Herbert, 1978). More precisely, a combination of lax discipline combined with hostile attitudes in the parents produces very aggressive and poorly controlled behaviour in the offspring. The lax parent is one who gives in to the child, acceding to his or her demands, indulging and allowing a great deal of freedom, being submissive and inconsistent, and, in extreme cases, neglecting and deserting the child. Parents with hosti attitudes are mainly unaccepting and disapproving of the child: they fail to give affection, understanding, or explanations to the child, and tend to use a lot of physical punishment but not to give reasons when they do exert their authority, which tends to be something applied erratically and unpredictably, not to mention arbitrarily. Over a long period of time this combination produces rebellious, irresponsible and aggressive children; they tend to be disorderly in the classroom, lacking in sustained concentration and irregular in their working habits.

The evidence suggests that children model their behaviour on that of their parents. Bandura and Walters (1959) compared families of adolescents who exhibited repetitive antisocial behaviour with those of boys who were neither markedly aggressive nor passive. It was found that the families differed in the extent to which they trained their sons to be aggressive through precept and example. Parents of the non-aggressive boys did not condone aggression to settle disputes, whereas the parents of the aggressive boys repeatedly modelled and reinforced combative attitudes and behaviour.

Contemporary influences

People rarely show aggression in blind, indiscriminate ways. Rather, aggressive actions tend to occur at certain times, in certain settings, towards certain objects or individuals, and in response to certain forms of provocation. People become aggressive at certain times because of current conditions and influences. There are two categories of contemporary influence to consider in planning treatment: contemporary circumstances which <u>instigate</u> aggression (viz. physical or verbal attacks, deprivation, frustration, conflict, and exposure to aggressive models), and those which <u>maintain</u> aggression (viz. direct, vicarious and self-reinforcement). The interactions between parents and child go a long way (as we have seen) toward shaping aggressive behaviour because of the inherent rewarding and reinforcing consequences. The child is likely to generalize what he or she learns about the utility and benefits of aggression to other situations. In these circumstances he or she has to put to the test the consequences of being aggressive. For example, he or she may try being aggressive (because it produced results with his siblings) with the peer group in the playground at school.

Learning and performance

A distinction must be made between the direct and vicarious learning experiences that contribute to the acquisition of aggressive behaviour, and those contemporary influences which determine whether the child will actually perform the behaviour he or she has acquired (Bandura, 1973). Aggres behaviour which has been acquired may not be performed, either because appropriate instigating conditions do not occur, or because the consequences of aggression are likely to be unrewarding or unpleasant.

Perhaps the most obvious instigating conditions for aggression are various forms of aversive experience, such as physical assaults, verbal threats or insults, and any frustrating conditions which prevent the child from getting what he or she wants. Although such aversive experiences do sometimes instigate aggression, this is not always the case. The anger they evoke may be accompanied by aggression or by other alternative responses.

In addition to aversive experiences, various incentives may also act as instigators of aggressive behaviour. Here, the instigation is the pull of expected reward rather than the push of aversive experience. Thus, aggressive and alternative responses are selected for performance on the basis of their anticipated consequences.

The probable nature of these consequences is conveyed to the child by means of various informational cues or discriminative stimuli. For instance, he or she might be told that acceptance into a gang depends on the successful performance of a certain aggressive act, or the presence of a weak potential victim may facilitate aggression, whereas a stronger victim might be conducive to an alternative response.

Finally, the contribution of exemplary models to the acquisition of aggressive behaviour was considered above, and such models also influence the performance of previously learned aggressive responses. In the first place, models who behave aggressively may be emulated by children. Conversely, aggression can be reduced in observers by exposure to models who behave in a non-aggressive fashion in the face of provocation.

Turning to the maintenance of aggressive behaviour, this is largely dependent on its consequences. Aggressive actions that are rewarded tend to be repeated, whereas those that are unrewarded or punished are generally discarded.

Patterson (1982) has developed the concept of a 'coercion' process to describe the event whereby other people interacting with the child become involved in supplying reinforcers for aggressive behaviours. They postulate negative reinforcement as a mechanism to strengthen the behaviour of the aggressor and, in some instances, of the victim as well. It is also hypothesized that some exchanges become extended and that when this occurs there is likely to be an escalation in the intensity of the painful stimuli. It is assumed that family systems which permit behaviour control by the use of pain are quite likely to produce children who exhibit high rates of noxious responses. Patterson (1982) observes that negative reinforcement is most likely to operate in certain closed social systems where the child must learn to cope with aversive stimuli. In such a family, for example, a boy's aggressive behaviour will be supported by both positive and negative reinforcement. His hitting terminates much of the aversive stimulation. In addition, as many as a quarter to a third of his coercive behaviours are likely to receive positive reinforcement for deviant behaviour as well.

Temperament

Some children seem temperamentally predisposed to develop difficult, unsocial behaviour. Early learning is shaped in such a way that the range of coercive tactics (crying, screaming, wilful tantrums, non-compliance) which are common to all young children, are not relinquished in this kind of child as he or she grows older - because of the way in which such behaviour has been mismanaged (Herbert, 1978).

Most parents, with little or no training - and I believe parenting to be in large part a skill - rear their children into broadly pro-social, norm-abiding adults (with the help of other socializing agents). There seems to be a fair amount of latitude in learning conditions for the child with an intact central nervous system, healthy body and a relatively un-volcanic temperament. For them, parental inconsistency, double-binds, unclear rules, etc., seem no more than a minor hindrance in the business of growing up. For others, predisposed to problem formation by handicaps, temperament lability, or learning deficits, a more predictable and persistent learning environment becomes essential. The demand characteristics of such children - the high rate, high intensity behaviours of a coercive kind so often associated with handicap - sadly (and too often) shape up an environment which is fraught, unpredictable and unpersevering!

Low self-esteem

Given the low self-esteem and under-achievement commonly found in conduct-disordered youngsters, it is worth bearing in mind (in planning an intervention) a potent source of reinforcement for aggressive behaviour - the aggressor him- or herself. To some extent children regulate their actions by self-produced consequences. They tend to repeat behaviour which has given them feelings of satisfaction and worth, conversely they tend to refrain from behaviour that produces self-criticism or other forms of self-devaluation.

Finally, aversive consequences (punishments) are another contemporary influence on the maintenance of aggressive behaviour. In general they tend to decrease aggression but their effects are complex and often paradoxical.

Conceptual framework

A conceptual framework for our work with families (Herbert, 1981) is summarized in figure 1. It is essentially a social learning approach to assessment and treatment. Here is the kind of information (some of which I've sketched in very briefly) we would be seeking with the family's help.

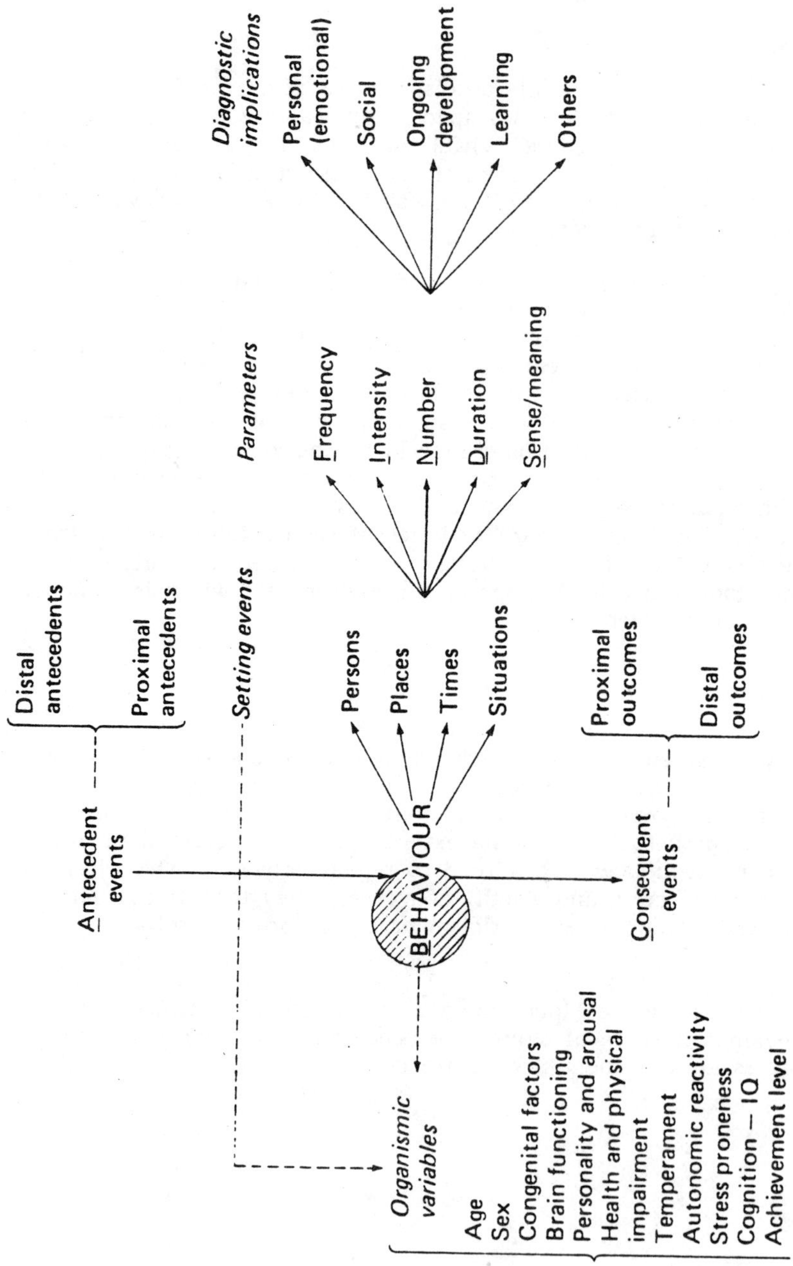

Figure 1. Factors in behavioural analysis

During the initial interview with the child and both parents (a crucial therapeutic configuration we have found in families where there are two parents), we explain who we are and how we work. It is CTRU policy to raise some of the major issues generated by a triadic behavioural approach: the concept of a genuine therapeutic partnership; our desire to share our knowledge and thinking with the parents, to take into account their own expertise based on long-standing knowledge of the child; and also to communicate the commitment we have to look at the ethical implications of any plans to institute changes within the family. There is a technical pay-off in sharing information, namely a reduction in the number of drop-outs from treatment (Baekeland and Lundwall, 1975). There may, however, be crucial variables in the style of training (for example, didactic versus a participant approach) which influence drop-out rates.

In all there are 20 assessment and treatment steps (Herbert, 1981). Parents frequently tell us at the debriefing interviews that this information and the 'insights' they gain from a more rigorous definition (and monitoring) of antisocial and prosocial behaviour, mark the beginning of change in their interactions with their child and (for some) a growing sense of competence. The baseline period is seldom therapeutically inert. About 10 per cent show reductions in target behaviours during the baseline period and maintain the improvement, at least over the four weeks we keep in touch with them.

In initiating baseline work, our preliminary task is to specify precisely what the allegedly maladaptive behaviours are, defining them in terms of their frequency, intensity, number and duration, and the meaning (or sense) they have for the child (FINDS), as shown in figure 1. The analysis is very much (but not exclusively) focused on what is called the 'ABC' sequence.

An analysis is made (by ourselves and the parents) of environmental conditions (and physical factor) leading up to, and immediately preceding the occurrence of the problem behaviour, and those that follow the performance of such behaviour. In this way we try to discover the antecedent stimuli (A) and consequences (C) which serve as eliciting or discriminative stimuli and thus trigger and maintain problem behaviour (B) in terms of learning and behavioural principles which will be understandable to the family.

The literature on behaviour modification - as it applies to children's conduct disorders - reflects a relative neglect of antecedent events. In their preoccupation with consequences of behaviour and, hence, operant procedures, behaviour modifiers sometimes overlook environmental controlling stimuli and the possibilities of ameliorating and restructuring the child's environment. It is helpful to observe what behaviours the parents model (consciously or unconsciously) for the child to imitate, or the confusing or weak verbal signals they give. There are other factors to be taken into account, but there is insufficient space here to elaborate (see Herbert, 1981).

The necessary basis for an individualized programme is a thorough behavioural analysis leading to a formulation which includes specification of the child's aggressive behaviour, some hypotheses about the contemporary factors that influence its instigation and maintenance, and an appraisal of the resources available for its treatment. On the basis of this formulation the goals of the intervention are chosen and the treatment plan is drawn up. Assuming that some intervention is considered to be necessary, then its goals are likely to be specified within the general framework of the prevention or reduction of aggressive behaviour and the promotion of more acceptable alternatives. Whenever possible a therapeutic contract is negotiated which specifies goals that are mutually agreeable to the child, the adults caring for him or her, and perhaps other people or institutions such as a court of law. The treatment plan provides the therapist with a strategy of intervention but his or her personal ingenuity and experience are the main resources for its implementation.

Once we have arrived at a formulation of the problem a detailed plan is made with the parents for the intervention, which they initiate. It is vital to warn them, if one is not to lose them, that the child is likely to get worse before he or she gets better - the post extinction burst. The 'machiavellian' is expert at producing target behaviour criterion confusion or slippage. A fairly intensive input at the beginning of a programme (providing prompts, cues, moral support, modelling, etc.) has proved invaluable in facilitating the work. We work basically with a family system: the child is viewed as part of a complex network of interacting social systems, any aspect of which may have a bearing on his or her present troubles.

Family discussion

We encourage family discussions in our work. It is helpful, as children get older, to hold family meetings in order to decide important family concerns such as agreements or contracts and to review matters of importance to the child; for example discipline, rules, pocket money, bedtime or when to return home from a party. Children are privy to all aspects of their therapeutic programmes.

Parents and significant others are trained to give instructions and use reinforcement effectively, and family members are encouraged to negotiate compromises and to bring about positive changes in ways other than by sheer coercion. This type of work can also involve communication training.

Therapeutic methods

The methods elaborated at the Unit (Herbert, 1981) involve a multifaceted package, depending for its final shape on the behavioural assessment. It might involve developmental and/or personal counselling. The procedures are not applied in a cookbook fashion! Variations in family values and attitudes, and individual differences in children require the flexibility of individualized programmes.

Antecedent control

There are several methods for reducing aggression based on a modification of the antecedent side of the ABC 'equation'.

1. STIMULUS CHANGE: REDUCING DISCRIMINATIVE STIMULI FOR AGGRESSION
The absence of the mother from the playroom may be a cue for the eldest child that threatening or hitting his younger brother is likely to gain him certain advantages, such as the best toys. In other words, certain stimulus conditions provide signals to the child that aggressive behaviour is likely to have rewarding consequences for him. Treatment programmes can be planned to reduce discriminative stimuli for such aggression.

2. PROVIDING MODELS FOR NON-AGGRESSIVE BEHAVIOUR

Acceptable alternatives to aggression may be enhanced by exposing youngsters to prestigious or influential individuals who manifest such alternative behaviours, especially when they are instrumental in obtaining rewards for these models.

3. REDUCING THE EXPOSURE TO AGGRESSIVE MODELS

We have already seen that there is evidence that exposure to other people behaving aggressively may facilitate the imitation of such behaviour by the observer. An attempt to reduce the exposure of a child to such aggressive models (for example, parents' behaviour) is likely to decrease the likelihood of him or her behaving similarly.

4. REDUCING AVERSIVE STIMULI

Violent reactions may be instigated by a large variety of aversive stimuli, by conflict, by physical assaults, by words of a threatening or humiliating nature, and by deprivation of the child's proper care, rights, and opportunities. It is reasonable to expect that a reduction of such aversive stimuli might be accompanied by a decrease in aggression. One technique is to resolve conflicts before they flare up into violence. Another technique involves the defusing of aversive stimuli by diminishing their power to arouse anger in the child. This can be achieved by using desensitization procedures.

5. DESENSITIZATION

Therapeutic procedures involving desensitization can also include the use of desensitization with cognitive relaxation, and desensitization in the absence of relaxation training. O'Donnell and Worell (1973) provide examples of the effectiveness of all three procedures applied in order to reduce anger.

6. SELF-INSTRUCTION

A technique that has proved invaluable with hyperactive, impulsive children is self-instruction training - the development of children's skills in guiding their own performance by the use of self-suggestion, comments, praise, and other directives. With the older children we tend to use more cognitively orientated methods (see Herbert, 1981), including self-control training (assertion and relaxation training, role play, behaviour rehearsal), problem solving skill training and social skill training.

7. COGNITIVE CHANGE (WITH REGARD TO ANTECEDENT EVENTS)

The performance of aggressive behaviour and its alternatives may be determined by the child's thought processes as well as his or her external environment. For example, the instigation of aggression may be influenced by antecedent cognitive events such as aversive thoughts (for example, remembering a past grudge), being aware of the probable consequences of aggressive actions, or being capable of solving problems mentally instead of 'lashing out' reflexly.

The youngster's search for various possible courses of action in the face of provocation and frustration can be made more flexible by attention to the thinking processes that precede, accompany and follow violent actions. A skill that hostile children sometimes lack is the ability to identify the precursors (labelling) to an aggressive outburst, so that they can bring into play more adaptive solutions to their problems.

Modifying a child's cognitions concerning an unpleasant experience might reduce its probability of triggering violent behaviour. To take an example, if the incident of another child knocking over the potential aggressor is redefined as an accident rather than an attack, there may be less risk of pugnacious reaction.

The influence of pleasant or aversive consequences on a child's actions are enhanced by his or her awareness of these consequences. Thus increasing a child's consciousness of the penalties contingent upon aggressive behaviour may reduce its performance.

There is evidence that the performance of aggressive acts is influenced by cognitive problem-solving processes. The processes which often precede and guide subsequent overt behaviour are as follows:

(a) being able to recognize problematic situations when they occur;
(b) making an attempt to resist the temptation to act impulsively or to do nothing to deal with the situation;
(c) defining the situation in concrete or operational terms and then formulating the major issues to be coped with;
(d) generating a number of possible responses which might be pursued in this situation;
(e) deciding on the course(s) of action most likely to result in positive consequences;
(f) finally, acting upon the final decision and verifying the effectiveness of the behaviour in resolving the problematic situation.

To facilitate the problem-solving process in children, they require help in identifying their aggressive behaviour and recognizing the conditions which provoke and maintain it. The problem situation is analysed, broken down into its component parts, and (hopefully) represented in a manner most likely to lead to a solution. A number of procedures are available for this purpose; they include self-recording by children of their hostile activities, together with their observations of the circumstances in which they occurred and their consequences. This information is used to show children the relationships between their behaviour and its controlling conditions.

8. CONFLICT RESOLUTION

Kifer et al. (1974) observe that one of the factors contributing to the delinquency of many youths is their inability to cope with conflict situations with authority figures. Conflict situations are defined by the authors as interpersonal situations in which the youth and an authority figure (such as a parent or teacher) have opposing desires. The youth may want to buy a motorbike, but his mother wants him to purchase an old car because she thinks bikes are dangerous and will get him into bad company. Youngsters often make inappropriate responses to conflict situations (such as fighting, withdrawing, tantrums, or destructive behaviour); an escalation of the conflict may bring them into contact with clinics, courts, and other agencies.

Negotiation could sometimes defuse these situations and produce more acceptable consequences for both parties. There are two broad approaches to conflict resolution: arbitration or mediation of specific conflicts, and modification of communication processes.

Behavioural contracting is the most common example of the arbitration approach. It involves the therapist in the role of a mediator or arbitrator who facilitates mutual agreements between opposing parties about reciprocal exchanges of specific behaviours and reinforcers.

Verbal instructions, practice and feedback are the major techniques used to modify communication processes. The emphasis of Kifer et al. (1974), for example, is entirely on learning new adaptive behaviours, rather than eliminating problem behaviours, and the techniques are primarily educational rather than therapeutic.

There is sound evidence that procedures based on selective reinforcement can reduce aggressive behaviour. In some studies aggressive behaviour is consistently ignored; in others it is ignored while a competing pattern of prosocial conduct is rewarded. In other cases prosocial behaviour is positively reinforced, but aggression is punished by removing the child from the scene (time-out).

Outcome control: extinction of aggressive behaviour

It should be possible to extinguish aggressive behaviour by discontinuing its reinforcing consequences if they can be identified. Planned ignoring may be utilized together with or instead of time-out and response-cost. Planned ignoring, time-out and response-cost have been systematically applied in programmes designed to provide stimulus conditions which signal to the child that his aggressive behaviour will not only fail to have rewarding consequences but, indeed, will result in punitive consequences. The provision of such discriminative stimuli may bring aggression under control while more acceptable alternative behaviour is being acquired.

Skills training

Bornstein et al. (1980) examined the effectiveness of social skills training with four highly aggressive children who were in-patients in a psychiatric setting. The children ranged in age from 8 to 12 years, were observed to manifest extreme levels of aggression with their peers, and were unable to express frustration and disappointment in an appropriate manner. More specifically, the children were found to exhibit a low rate of eye contact, an inability to make appropriate requests of others, and a high degree of hostile tone in their responses. These specific responses were measured on a series of role-play scenes.

Following pre-treatment assessment, children received three half-hour sessions of social skills training for each of the three targeted deficits observed in the role-play assessment. Training was first applied to eye contact, then to hostile tone, and finally to appropriate requests. Training consisted of instructions, feedback, modelling, behaviour rehearsal, and reinforcement. The therapist presented one of the interpersonal scenes and instructed the child on appropriate behaviour; the child performed the response; the therapist provided feedback and reinforcement; a confederate modelled the appropriate response; the therapist provided feedback, reinforcement, and new instructions to the child; the child rehearsed the response for several trials until the criteria for targeted response had been reached. Upon satisfactory performance, training proceeded in a similar fashion to new interpersonal situations. Throughout training, children were assessed on the role-play scenes approximately three times per week.

Elder et al. (1979) conducted a study with four highly aggressive, adolescent psychiatric patients but extended the test of generalization to untrained role-play scenes, natural settings and ward behaviour. Training was conducted in a group and in an on-ward classroom. Further, training was conducted four days per week for approximately 45 minutes per day for a total of fourteen sessions. Hence, training was extended; it was conducted in groups in a natural setting; and an attempt was made to assess generalization from a number of perspectives.

Training proceeded in a standard fashion and included instructions, feedback, modelling, behaviour rehearsal, and reinforcement. Results of the Bornstein et al. (1980) investigation indicated that positive effects of training were achieved for each target behaviour for each child. However, the changes noted in training did not generalize consistently to other settings. Thus, although the findings indicate that social skills training altered specific responses in specific role-play situations, the training did not generalize consistently to untrained prompts or to more natural situations. Still, the results of this study indicate that social skills training may be useful with aggressive children.

Results in the Elder et al. (1979) study indicated that social skills training highly effective and that all three targeted social skills were acquired by each of the adolescents. Generalization of the trained skills was evident in the untrained scenes and in the ward setting. The adolescents were observed to make fewer interruptions, to employ more appropriate responses to negative situations, and to make more appropriate requests of others. Furthermore, these changes in social skills were associated with ward changes.

There is little doubt that parents can be taught to use behavioural methods with their children and that for aggressive problems (and other disorders) they are effective (Herbert, 1978). As with the history of systematic desensitization, the main thrust of research is to discover the active therapeutic expedients in what are usually multi-element treatment packages, and the refinements which facilitate parent training. It must be admitted, however, that experience in both natural and residential homes tells us that behavioural solutions to aggressive, conduct disordered children has limitations. Because of the very nature of the families of many aggressive, pre-delinquent or delinquent young people, co-operation will not always be forthcoming from parents or caregivers. Implementation of treatment programmes may require very lengthy casework just to get to the point of a useful assessment, let alone to the consistency and application required of a challenging and tiring programme. The problem of temporal generalization is particularly acute with caregivers whose commitment is half-hearted. Results to date are sufficiently encouraging to make this a cautionary rather than pessimistic ending.

References

BAEKELAND, F. and LUNDWALL, L. (1975) Dropping out of treatment: A critical reivew. **Psychological Bulletin, 82,** 738-783

BANDURA, A. (1973) **Aggression: A social learning analysis.** Englewood Cliffs, NJ: Prentice-Hall

BANDURA, A. and WALTERS, R.H. (1959) **Adolescent Aggression.** New York: Ronald

BORNSTEIN, M.R., BELLACK, A.S. and HERSEN, M. (1980) Social skills training for highly aggressive children. **Behavior Modification, 4,** 173-186

ELDER, J.P., EDELSTEIN, B.A. and NARICK, M.M. (1979) Adolescent psychiatric patients: modifying aggressive behaviour with social skills training. **Behavior Modification, 3,** 161-178

FARRINGTON, D.P. (1979) Delinquent behaviour modification in the natural environment. **British Journal of Criminology, 19,** 353-372

HERBERT, M. (1978) **Conduct Disorders of Childhood and Adolescence.** Chichester: Wiley

HERBERT, M. (1981) **Behavioural Treatment of Problem Children: A practice manual.** London: Academic Press

HERBERT, M. (1985) **Caring for Your Children: A practical guide.** Oxford: Blackwell

KIFER, R.E., LEWIS, M.A., GREEN, D.R. and PHILLIPS, E.L. (1974) Training predelinquent youths and their parents to negotiate conflict situations. **Journal of Applied Behavior Analysis, 7,** 357-364

LEFKOWITZ, M.M., ERON, L.D. WALDER, L.O. and HEUSSMAN, L.R. (1977) **Growing Up To Be Violent.** Oxford: Pergamon

O'DONNELL, C.R. and WORELL, L. (1973). Motor and cognitive relaxation in the desansitization of anger. **Behaviour Research and Therapy, 11,** 473-481

PATTERSON, G.R. (1982) **Coercive Family Process.** Eugene, Oreg: Castalia Publishing Company

ROBINS, L.N. (1966) **Deviant Children Grown-Up.** Baltimore: Williams & Wilkins

MANAGEMENT OF VIOLENCE IN A YOUTH TREATMENT CENTRE

M. Gentry and E.B. Ostapiuk

Introduction

Following a number of official enquiries in the mid and late 1960s which highlighted a lack of suitable provision for the most difficult and disturbed children of both sexes then contained in the child care system, plans were made to establish a new kind of residential treatment facility. It was envisaged that these new centres would provide a combination of security, intensive treatment, and long-term care for extremely difficult adolescents whose needs for containment and treatment were beyond the resources of local authorities, or who were detained under s53 of the Children and Young Persons Act 1933, having committed very serious offences. The newly designated Youth Treatment Centres (YTCs) were thus seen as being at the end of the spectrum of child care provision for the failures who might otherwise have been dealt with by the penal or Special Hospital systems.

The first Youth Treatment Centre, St Charles, in Brentwood, Essex was opened in 1971. The second, Glenthorne, in Birmingham, opened its doors in early 1978. These two centres are, thus far, the only two such 'last resort' facilities in the United Kingdom. Both are administered directly by the Children Maternity and Prevention (CMP) Division of the Department of Health and Social Security and are independent of local authorities. They admit boys and girls aged between 10 and 19 years. A more detailed description of Glenthorne Youth Treatment Centre, its organization, client group and treatment programmes, is given in an earlier paper by Ostapiuk and Westwood (1986). Whereas the first YTC, St Charles, adopted a psychodynamic approach to treatment, Glenthorne decided to apply a broadly behavioural framework to the management and treatment of a wide range of adolescent referral problems. Although the choice of a behavioural model was a democratic one, taken by the early staff group at the Centre, rather than a policy directive from above, there were a number of important rationales which underlined the decision. First, in a new establishment there was a clear need for an explicit, readily understood framework within which to operate. Second, the system had to provide unambiguous boundaries both for staff and clients; firm, though realistic, expectations for achievement; and a fair and consistently applied set of consequences for rule breaking or failure to meet expectations. Third, and most important, the system had to be positive in orientation, emphasizing both the intrinsic and the tangible gains of positive achievement rather than the negative aspects of failure.

Over the years the Centre has, in particular, attempted to apply the behavioural model to the management of violence and aggressive behaviour, since this has been part of a frequently recurring picture of disruption and failure for many of the young persons placed at Glenthorne YTC. This paper describes how violence in an institutional context has been tackled at Glenthorne YTC and how certain important decisions helped to conceptualize both the nature of the problem and what to do about it. In doing so we will follow the distinction which is often made between instrumental and angry violence (Buss, 1961). The former refers to the use of violence in a calculated way to achieve a particular goal, such as robbery. By contrast angry violence is impulsive and reflects a lack of control over strong emotional arousal. Youngsters are placed at YTCs on the basis of emotional and psychological disturbance and it is the second type of violence that is generally exhibited and which is the subject of this paper.

From problem to policy

From the outset it seemed important to make a clear distinction between the containment of aggressive or violent incidents as and when they occurred, and the longer term therapeutic input needed to treat violent and aggressive young persons. This distinction between control and containment on the one hand, and that of treatment on the other, suggested that clear guidelines were necessary if a coherent and consistently applied set of procedures were to operate successfully. A behavioural system which emphasizes observation and careful recording of data further prompted the need for an enabling framework of internal policy which addressed both of these issues. It was felt that there were several good reasons why this should be done.

First, it would allow the Centre to make a clear statement of its procedures and the rationales for their use, which should be open to both internal and public scrutiny. Second, it would serve to improve communication of information by specifying the kind of data that had to be recorded, how and when it was to be recorded and how it was to be passed on for scrutiny. Third, it would facilitate consistency of approach by specifying what to do, and how and when to do it, in the context of violent incidents. Fourth, it would have implications for the training of staff in handling incidents more effectively. Fifth, it would contribute to a supportive atmosphere by giving staff confidence in the knowledge that their colleagues will respond in expected and predictable ways in violent situations; the resultant effect would be to foster a tension-free, relaxed working atmosphere for both staff and young persons. Last, but not least, a clear framework should make the task of monitoring and evaluating the Centre's response to violence easier; this in turn would foster constructive feedback which would guard against complacency and the endemic problems of the 'hardening of institutional arteries'.

Figure 1. Factors in policy making

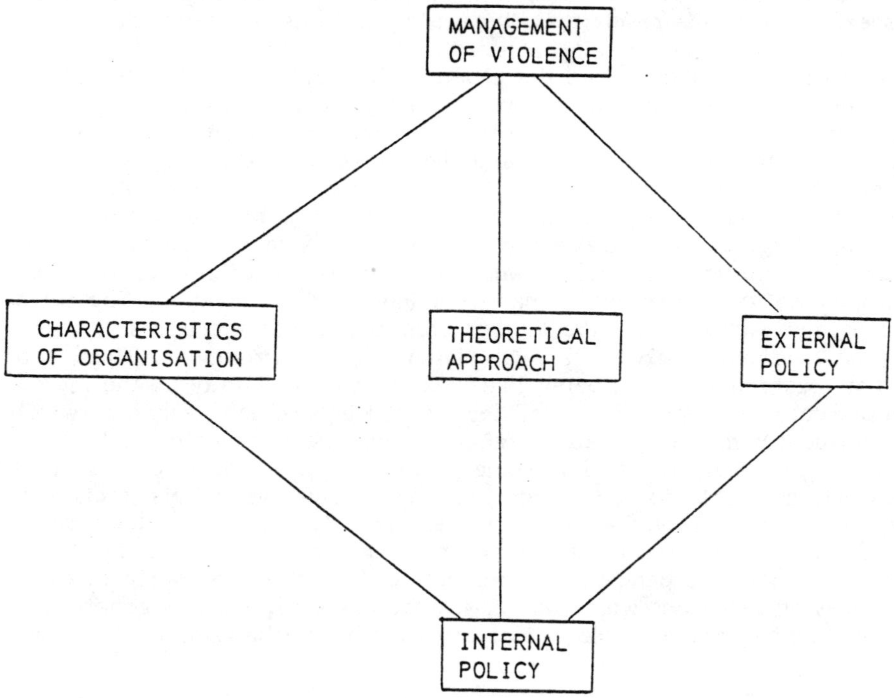

In formulating an internal policy for the management of violence there were three main factors which were taken into account (see figure 1), these were the characteristics of the organization or institution; the theoretical approach adopted by the organization; and external policy constraints.

The characteristics of an organization set the limits within which a policy will actually be operated. In any residential establishment the design of the building has a substantial influence on the behaviour of both staff and residents. An obvious feature in this context is the capacity to section off an area in which a violent incident occurs and the provision of individual secure rooms where someone can be contained. More generally, interior design and decoration can convey to residents something about the staff expectations of disruptive behaviour (for example, fixed furniture or plastic cutlery). Another important organizational feature is the staffing of the institution, including the staff to resident ratio, the type of staff and the expectations which senior management have of them. At Glenthorne YTC, each living unit accommodates up to 10 youngsters who are cared for by a staff team of 12 groupworkers, a Unit Leader and his or her deputy. In addition, each unit receives psychology and social work support. Groupworkers are all qualified as residential child care officers, teachers or nurses. Each team is expected to produce a good level of care and to achieve specific treatment goals with each youngster. In addition, each team is expected to develop their overall care and treatment programme and not become complacent. Glenthorne YTC has links with Leicester University and each year six groupworkers are sent on the Diploma Course in Applied Social Learning Theory and Practice.

The adoption of a single theoretical approach is necessary in an organization in which the primary agents of treatment are care workers who must work together as a team. There has been an increase in the development of the multidisciplinary approach to the treatment of people with psychological problems on the basis that no single profession can provide a comprehensive service. While there are clearly advantages in such professional collaboration it is sometimes difficult to reconcile different perspectives with the result that there is an absence of an overall philosophy. The social learning approach which has been adopted at Glenthorne YTC comes within the broad area of behavioural psychology. The main focus of attention is observable behaviour and the purpose of treatment is to achieve some definite behavioural change. Assessment is mainly concerned with current behaviour and the environmental factors which contribute to its occurrence, although past influences are also examined in order to determine how particular behaviour patterns have developed. Behavioural approaches are based on the hypothesis that much of a person's behaviour is learned, maintained and regulated by the effects of environmental consequences of that behaviour to the individual. The social learning approach supports the further proposition that there is a reciprocal influence between individuals and their environment. Thus, people are not regarded either as being like weather vanes, totally at the mercy of environmental influences or as if they existed in a social vacuum in which such influences do not operate. Social learning theorists maintain that there are four main types of learning which are important processes in human behaviour: classical, operant, cognitive and observational. This is distinct from more radical behavioural approaches and reflects the development of behavioural theory over the last 20 years (Bandura, 1969; 1977a; 1977b; Mischel, 1973). This perspective does not exclude the importance of other influences on behaviour which are of a different kind, such as genetic or organic factors. For example, there are specific mechanisms in the brain which have been shown to be associated with aggressive behaviour in both humans and animals (Avis, 1974). Biological factors which influence the development of aggressive behaviour in children are also acknowledged, but the ability to perform specific acts must be acquired either by observation of other people (Bandura, 1965; 1977a) or by direct experience, i.e. through the process of learning. The maintenance of aggressive behaviour is very largely dependent on its consequences, in that aggressive behaviour which is rewarded will tend to recur and aggressive behaviour which is either not rewarded or punished will diminish.

The adoption of a behavioural approach as the main component of treatment implies the acceptance of individual/environmental interaction as being the most promising area for consideration in order to achieve a long term change in an individual's behaviour. A specific example of the difference between behavioural and some other approaches which is often noted is the role of insight (Herbert, 1981; Yelloly, 1972). Insight can certainly produce changes in attitude and behaviour but behaviour therapists do not regard it as being a primary means of achieving therapeutic goals. Rather, there is evidence that insight which seems apparent from what a person says during the course of therapy frequently follows rather than precedes behavioural change (Cautela, 1965; Yelloly, 1972). Within this framework some behaviourists (Owens and Walter, 1980) have claimed that a behavioural psychotherapy is possible whereby behaviour change is brought about by appropriate verbal guidance with respect to environmental contingencies. Thus, it is accepted that instruction and counselling are valid methods of producing behaviour change in the absence of the manipulation of reinforcement or punishment which operant behaviourists would regard as essential.

External policy considerations are no less importnat in shaping the ethos and practice of child care in an institution. The Child Care Act (1980) and Secure Accommodation (No. 2) Regulations (1983), specifically the criteria for placement of a child in a single separation room, made it clear that certain practices which had previously gone unquestioned were now unacceptable. It became necessary to provide official justification for certain courses of action and meet specific criteria in order not only to detain a young person in security but to use the obvious physical aspects of security (i.e. locking a child in a room) to contain violent and aggressive behaviour.

Such external guidelines prompted Glenthorne YTC to re-examine its existing practice. Where possible an attempt was made to comply not only with the letter of the law but also the spirit. The Centre's policy on handling violent incidents, in line with the DHSS circular on management of violent hospital patients (DHSS, 1976), had to be clarified. As a result, the Centre's earlier rejection of medication as a means of control was reaffirmed. Time-out was carefully defined and its application tightly prescribed,it was to be seen as an individualized and carefully considered consequences rather than a standard penalty for disruptive, non-complaint behaviour. It was further emphasized that time-out (a treatment procedure) should not be operated in separation rooms designated for the purpose of containing a violent person (a management/control procedure).

These are only some of the issues addressed in an attempt to achieve a balance between narrow compliance with regulations on the one hand and a flexible and responsive system that recognized individual differences in violent responses.

Containment and control

Containment and control of violent incidents as they occur is a prerequisite for the successful, longer-term treatment of young persons with aggressive tendencies. Institutional and management needs for control and, initially at least, compliance with prerequisites for the smooth functioning of an organization were seen as important factors to be taken into account when establishing a coherent policy for managing violence. This need for clearly stated boundaries implies that young persons must experience firm external control from the day they are admitted to the Centre. The amount of external control applied and the rate at which it is gradually released will depend not only upon the characteristics of the client and the severity of the client's presenting problem (these issues will be discussed in the section on treatment) but also upon official guidelines concerning detention of persons in secure conditions (i.e. Child Care Act 1980; Secure Accommodation (No. 2) Regulations, 1983), and in-house regulations and codes of practice.

Following lengthy discussions at Glenthorne YTC in the summer of 1983, an outline policy for handling violent incidents was produced which attempted to integrate both official guidelines and existing procedures into a unified code of practice forming part of the Centre's 'Procedures Manual'. The following are a summary of the salient points.

1. Modifying violent behaviour was to be considered of primary importance in the Centre's treatment programmes, both for the sake of young persons and staff. Recognizing that violent responses to stress were often the main reason for placing young persons in the secure conditions of a Youth Treatment Centre, the Centre viewed the modification of violent behaviour and the learning of alternatives to be an important factor in the progress of young persons towards discharge and freedom. Whilst staff at the centre were to expect to receive much of the angry and aggressive responses which the young person had previously learned elsewhere, there were limits to the behaviour which staff could tolerate even as alternatives were being learned. For the safety of all in the Centre it had to be made clear that physical assault was as unacceptable here as it was in the outside world. Thus the response of staff to serious incidents had to be immediate and uncompromising, requiring the necessary procedures to be clearly understood so that the risk of injury to those involved be minimized.

2. The routine response to violent behaviour would be removal of the young person to a room specifically designated for the purpose of containing the person safely (termed a Separation Room).

3. Whenever a young person was to be placed in a Separation Room a senior manager had to be informed immediately.

4. The young person would remain in a Separation Room only as long as physical containment was necessary and would be checked at last every 15 minutes.

5. All incidents involving use of Separation Rooms had to be fully described on appropriate forms.

6. Separation Rooms were not to be used as a means of punishing the young person who had been violent, but as a means of containing the violence safely. The guidelines also emphasized the need to intervene early and always attempt to use appropriate alternatives to diffuse potentially violent situations. Here the existing behavioural management systems already in use could be drawn upon to avoid escalation of the incident (such as use of a fixed penalty, for example, an early bedtime; a drop to a lower privilege level; use of time-out, etc.)

The acronym 'ACT' (see figure 2), serves as a guide to staff which emphasizes the positive response required to manage violence effectively. It prompts staff to anticipate problem situations by paying attention to the chain of events which typically results in conflict and violence, and to avoid escalation by early and well-judged intervention. It further suggests the need to take firm control of the situation by being decisive and positive in one's actions, and to contain the young person's behaviour thus minimizing damage to property or injury to people. The need to train staff in the correct procedures for dealing with violence is also made clear. Familiarity with proper restraint procedures, writing up the details of incidents and providing constructive feedback to staff on their handling of violent incidents should form the basis of a training package which is continuously monitored and updated as recommended procedures change. Finally, the young person's behavioural excesses and deficits which relate to violence and aggression must be treated. The object of a combined management and treatment strategy for violence is to return the young person to the outside world better able to deal with stress and frustration without resorting to violence. Thus, in the long term, there must be a gradual shift away from external, institutional control towards the young person's exercise of learned self-control. Achieving this transition is dealt with in the next section concerning treatment.

Figure 2. ACT - positive management of violence

A	ANTICIPATE	-	the problem
	AVOID	-	escalation
C	CONTROL	-	the situation
	CONTAIN	-	the behaviour
T	TRAIN	-	staff
	TREAT	-	client

Treatment

Persistent violent behaviour will result in a young person effectively marking time and not progressing through the Centre. It is essential that youngsters are consistently rewarded for good behaviour and either not rewarded or punished for unacceptable behaviour. This simple statement of good practice cannot be achieved in an institution unless an organized system of observation and recording is maintained together with an effective contingency management system. This system has been described elsewhere (Ostapiuk and Westwood, 1986).

On the admission unit the youngsters live within a strict regime in which there is a high level of external control by staff. As youngsters progress through the Centre they are gradually encouraged to monitor their own behaviour and maintain a good level of socially acceptable behaviour without external restraints being imposed by staff. This shift in control is crucial to the broad aim of treatment which is to enable youngsters to develop sufficient self-control and self-management to return to the community and live in a socially acceptable way.

The treatment process involves the following stages:

1. Assessment

Incidents of violent behaviour committed by a youngster both at the centre and prior to admission are recorded and described in detail. The basic framework for the descriptions is shown in figure 3.

Figure 3. The ABC of assessment

ANTECEDENTS ——→ BEHAVIOUR ——→ CONSEQUENCES

Personal / Situational (Antecedents)　　Short Term / Long Term (Consequences)

Contributing factors to the violent incidents (Antecedents), the exact nature of the incidents (Behaviour) and what happened afterwards (Consequences) are recorded. Particular attention is paid to the frequency, intensity and duration of violent incidents over a period of time. All the assessment information is examined and an overall functional analysis produced in which an attempt is made to explain an individual youngster's pattern of behaviour.

2. Selection of target behaviours

The results of the assessment are discussed with the youngster concerned, who will be encouraged to make a commitment to reducing/eliminating the occurrence of violent behaviour and to co-operate in a plan of treatment to achieve this goal. Most youngsters are unsure about their desire to change or their ability to do so. The combination of observing other youngsters making progress through the Centre by behaving well, and individual counselling aimed at increasing motivation to change, usually results in youngsters taking an active part in their treatment (see Miller, 1983, for a discussion of motivational interviewing). Since the main aim of treatment is the development of self-control by youngsters themselves, targets are usually described in terms of developing alternative patterns of behaviour to violence which will have the same function. A youngster who experiences a build-up of physical tension very quickly in response to mild provocation and releases the tension in an aggressive manner would be encouraged to develop other ways of reducing this tension in a non-violent way. For another youngster the main target might be persistent aggressive thought which resulted in him or her becoming increasingly tense over a period of time and eventually directing aggression towards an innocent victim. Feldman (1977) has drawn attention to the selection of treatment goals which primarily benefit an institution and do not reflect either the reason for an individual's admission or future placement. For example, emphasis may be placed on compliance within the routine of the institution and being a 'model inmate', which does not prepare someone for return to the community. Further, while it is more constructive to encourage achievement in educational and occupational activities, undue emphasis on these areas can result in lack of attention being paid to more important areas.

The distinction between under-controlled and over-controlled individuals is a useful one in this context (Megargee, 1966). An under-controlled person will tend to exhibit aggressive behaviour in response to relatively minor provocation and, therefore, will do so quite frequently. The problem is quite obvious and is not likely to be overlooked in discussions about treatment. By contrast, an over-controlled person will behave aggressively less frequently but any aggression will usually be quite intense. An over-controlled youngster may have committed a serious assault which caused him or her to be admitted but not behave aggressively at all within an insitutional environment. It would be quite wrong to ignore this area simply because the youngster did not cause any immediate management problems.

3. **Selection of treatment methods**

There are numerous combinations of treatment strategies which can be applied within the social learning framework and which have been summarized elsewhere (for example, Herbert, 1981). A brief description of an individual case is given below which illustrates both the general approach and some particular treatment methods.

CASE STUDY
Mark was a 17-year-old lad who had a history of minor assaults against boys of similar age. These were typically sudden outbursts during which he used his fists and then ran away. Sometimes he had himself been injured during the fights. He was generally described as having a quick temper but usually calmed down quite soon. He got angry when prevented from doing what he wanted when he wanted. He was particularly sensitive to comments about his family, who lived in a poor area of the city and who were well known to the local police and social services. He said that when he got angry he could not think clearly and felt physically very tense. After an outburst he felt more relaxed but often regretted what he had done. Most of his peers were wary of him and he appeared to enjoy being regarded as someone not to cross. He was of average intelligence.

A very simple functional analysis identifed three important antecedents to Mark's violent behaviour:

(a) frustration in doing what he wants immediately;
(b) sensitiveness to negative comments about his family;
(c) a high level of emotional arousal which could build up very quickly.

His violence was limited to using his fists and a detailed record of outbursts within the Centre described other relevant variables (frequency, duration, and so forth). The consequences of his violence were:

(a) release of physical tension;
(b) occasional regret;
(c) occasional physical injury;
(d) reinforcement of a tough self-image due to the reaction of some of his peers;
(e) negative consequences within the regime of the Centre.

Commitment to treatment was only achieved after three months of individual counselling, during which Mark stopped saying that he was only 'serving time' and began to discuss the short- and long-term negative consequences of his violent behaviour. Three treatment targets were then identified and agreed with Mark:

(a) To improve his ability to deal with conflict situations. It was evident from discussions with Mark that even when he was calm he was unable to assert himself with another youngster or member of staff in an appropriate way. He had not developed the ability to put forward his own point of view appropriately in a non-threatening way. This goal was successfully achieved in role play situations as part of an individual assertivenes training programme.

(b) To reduce the quick and intense anger which he experienced. Even when the first target had been achieved and Mark began to use his new skills in actual situations outside the training sessions, there were still a number of occasions when he became so angry that he was unable to apply these skills. He no longer used violence but would storm out of the difficult situation and leave matters unresolved.

After much discussion it was decided to teach him a self-instruction strategy, which would effectively enable him to 'talk himself out of his anger' and remain calm enough to use his assertive skills. He was taught to be aware of the physical signs of angry arousal and to implement this strategy as soon as possible. Briefly, Mark chose a few statements which had most meaning for him, from a list which was given to him, for example, 'I have handled worse situations than this'. Mark was very pleased with the progress that he made and began to talk about 'beating his anger' and 'being in control'. These were clear signs that the shift in control from external institutional constraints, to self-control was taking place.

(c) To reduce his sensitivity to comments about his family. This was achieved by means of a process of desensitization in individual sessions during which he was exposed to negative comments about his family made by a member of staff. This was carried out using a simple five-point hierarchy of increasingly distasteful comments for Mark and working through the list from the mildest to the strongest. He also developed appropriate responses to such comments which allowed him to feel that he had not simply stood back and allowed his family to be criticized.

Conclusions

The approach to the management of violent behaviour which has been outlined in this paper has been developed over a period of seven years in one particular institution. During this time some basic principles have been found to be important and may be relevant to other settings.

The distinction between containment and treatment is essential in a closed institution. Staff who deal directly with violent incidents benefit from operating within a framework which emphasizes the difference between two sets of procedures which are intended to achieve different goals.

Containment procedures must be simple and unambiguous because they will be put into effect when staff are under stress. It is essential that staff have support both during and after violent incidents. However, in addition to measures which provide guidance and support, there also needs to be a monitoring system so that staff are clearly accountable for their actions and in order that any deficiencies in the policy are recorded. It is important that procedures which may be necessary for short-term containment, such as a youngster being confined to a locked room, are not confused with treatment procedures with which they have some similarity, such as time-out.

Successful treatment of well-established patterns of violent behaviour is not easy to achieve and it is important that the particular treatment model which is adopted is clearly specified. This is especially true when the individual clients are in contact with a number of different care staff who need to be consistent in their approach. The social learning model which forms the theoretical basis of the treatment at Glenthorne YTC has proved to be very useful in the development of practical and effective methods of achieving substantial modification of violent behaviour. It has led to a system of explicit treatment planning which incorporates goals and methods based on thorough assessment. The monitoring of progress occurs at weekly treatment meetings on every youngster and comprehensive reviews every three months. In this way, both staff and youngsters receive regular and detailed feedback about progress and problems which develop are noted and dealt with almost immediately.

References

AVIS, H. (1974) The neuropharmacology of aggression. **Psychological Bulletin, 81,** 47-63

BANDURA, A. (1965) Behavioural modifications through modelling procdures. In: L. Krasner and L. Ullman (eds) **Research in Behavior Modification.** New York: Holt, Rinehart & Winston

BANDURA, A. (1969) **Principles of Behavior Modification.** New York: Holt, Rinehart & Winston

BANDURA, A. (1977a) **Social Learning Theory.** Englewood Cliffs, NJ: Prentice Hall

BANDURA, A. (1977b) Self-efficacy - towards a unifying theory of behavioural change. **Psychological Review, 84,** 191-215

BUSS, A. (1961) **The Psychology of Aggression.** Chichester: Wiley

CAUTELA, J. (1965) Desensitization and insight. **Behavior Research and Therapy, 3,** 59-64

DHSS (1976) **The Management of Violent or Potentially Violent Hospital Patients.** Health Circular (II), Health Services Management. London: HMSO

DHSS (1980) **Child Care Act 1980.** London: HMSO

DHSS (1983) **Secure Accommodation (No. 2) Regulations 1983.** London: HMSO.

FELDMAN, P. (1977) **Criminal behaviour: A psychological analysis.** Chichester: Wiley

HERBERT, M. (1978) **Conduct Disorders of Childhood and Adolescence.** Chichester: Wiley

HERBERT, M. (1981) **Behavioural Treatment of Problem Children: A practice manual.** London: Academic Press

MEGARGEE, E. (1966) Undercontrolled and overcontrolled personality types in extreme antisocial aggression. **Psychological Monographs, 80,** Whole No. 611

MILLER, W. (1983) Motivational interviewing with problem drinkers. **Behavioural Psychotherapy, 11,** 147-172

MISCHEL, W. (1973) Toward a cognitive social learning reconceptualization of personality. **Psychological Review, 80,** 252-283

OSTAPIUK, E. and WESTWOOD, S. (1986) Glenthorne Youth Treatment Centre: working with adolescents in gradations of security. In: C. Hollin and K. Howells (eds) **Clinical Approaches to Criminal Behaviour. Issues in Criminological and Legal Psychology, No. 9.** Leicester: The British Psychological Society

OWENS, G. and WALTER, A.J. (1980) Naive behaviourism and behaviour modification. **Bulletin of The British Psychological Society, 33,** 312-314

YELLOLY, M. (1972) The concept of insight. In: D. Jehu (ed.) **Behaviour Modification in Social Work.** Chichester: Wiley

PREVENTING FACE-TO-FACE VIOLENCE

William Davies

Introduction

To some people, the idea that they might be assaulted by a patient or client is an extremely frightening one. We therefore need to be aware of the best ways of avoiding this happening, not only for our own peace of mind, but also so that we can continue more effectively with our main task, that of helping the patients or clients we work with.

Many of the ideas that are going to be presented are straightforward ones, very much in line with common sense. It might be slightly surprising, therefore, that many of them are also at variance with what is sometimes practised. It is best to consider them under a number of headings, as follows.

The model

The model to be used is this:

1. Violence is an interaction between two or more people; it is not something that resides in only one of the people involved in a fight.

2. Violence is not inevitable.

3. We are all sometimes prone to violence.

This contrasts with a frequently implied alternative model which suggests that Mr or Mrs X is a downright violent person because of some physiological process, there is nothing we can do about it, and they will always be like that.

The key statement then, is that violence is an interaction, and we can do something about it. The truth of the interactive nature of violence is demonstrated by studies such as that of Davies (1983), which revealed that experienced prison officers are less likely to be assaulted than inexperienced ones. If this is so, it cannot be that violence is simply something that resides in the aggressor. However, this is not to dispute that there are certainly some people who are more frequently involved in violent incidents than others.

Our attitudes

There are a variety of statements that staff say to themselves, many of which are not helpful. The following are some examples:

1. I must not let him get away with it.

2. I must stand up to him.

3. I must not show that I am afraid.

4. I must do something about this.

5. I should be able to deal with anyone.

6. He must be taught a lesson.

7. I must not run away.

8. I must not ask advice.

Some of these (for example, not running away) can have an immediate impact at the time of a particular violent incident. Others, such as not seeking advice or feeling that you must be able to deal with everyone, have a more insidious and long-term effect on future behaviour.

It is not feasible to say that certain attitudes are right or wrong, as we all work out our attitudes for ourselves. However, it is fair to make two comments: first, that some of these attitudes are more likely to lead to violent incidents than others, and second, that each of us needs to think about and determine our attitudes in advance of an incident arising. This way one is more likely to act in a way which one believes is correct, and less likely to act entirely on impulse.

Precautions worth taking

There are a range of basic precautions which, if they are systematically and regularly used, will eliminate a percentage of violent incidents. These are as follows:

1. When you are about to see somebody you know may be aggressive or violent do not see them alone, either in your office or elsewhere (domiciliary visit, etc.).

2. Make sure that the potentially violent person is aware that you are not alone - that there is someone else nearby in the building, in another office perhaps. This way you will utlilize any deterrent effect that the 'knowledge of reinforcement' has.

3. Notify colleagues that you are about to see a person who may be aggressive or violent, and agree in detail what they should do in a range of eventualities.

4. Find out as much information as you can about the potentially violent person, before seeing him or her. Specifically, find out what situations they are prone to be violent in. If the person in question is a regular client of yours make sure you have revised relevant information so that you avoid questions such as: 'What does your mother think of this?' having forgotten that his mother died six months previously. Needless to say such questions can be very antagonizing. Consider having alarm buzzers in your office if you regularly see aggressive people. The button should of course be discreet, and you should check regularly that it works. Most important perhaps is that other staff should know exactly what to do if the buzzer is activated. Should they come and try and rescue you? Or phone the police? Or what?

5. Agree a system for checking on the safety of staff in different offices. If you hear a disturbance coming from one office should you go and investigate or will this spoil the relationship being developed? If you

decide on a system which involves phone calls, make sure that this involves 'closed' questions such as: 'do you want me to come in?' rather than open questions such as 'what is happening in there?' Plainly, the latter question is a very difficult one to answer.

6. Prevent waiting time as far as possible; clients and patients can wind themselves up considerably during this period. If they have to wait, try to engineer a situation which will make the time pass for them as easily as possible (with magazines, perhaps even coffee) and make an estimate as to how long they will be kept waiting. It is important not to make an under-estimate in the futile hope that the person will somehow not notice how long he or she has been kept waiting. Some people will work out their own solution, by leaving and coming back later.

7. Rehearse under what circumstances staff in your building should make an emergency call to the police. If your agency regularly sees aggressive clients, consider having a liaison officer allocated to you from the local station - someone who would take special interest in your situation and be able to maintain a regular link between you and the police.

8. Treat everyone with care and respect. It is surprising how much caring and respect can be engendered by physical threat. Don't push people into resorting to this.

9. If you know that the relationship between you and your client is not a good one, then consider transferring responsibility for him or her to a colleague. There is no reason why you should expect yourself to be able to deal with every client who presents. It is the responsibility of your profession rather than you personally, and clients can be transferred both from and to you.

10. Beware of various types of clothing such as ties which can be used for strangling you (there do exist clip-on ties which simply pull off under force), long hair and earrings.

11. When walking upstairs, go in front of the client; when walking downstairs, follow behind. As with all such measures it is important simply to establish the habit of using them, and not employ them as elaborate, suspicion-laden techniques which make the client ill at ease.

12. In a potentially violent situation, get uninvolved people out of the way, in order both to avoid harm coming to them, and to minimize any loss of face or 'audience' effects.

13. It is important not to be prejudiced against a client or unduly suspicious about him or her, simply because of information that has been passed to you. For example, a receptionist may tell you that a particular person is agitated, and this is useful to know so long as you do not react adversely and produce a self-fulfilling prophecy.

14. If you are transporting someone in your car, it is usually best to have them in the front with you. This prevents them attacking you from behind, although not of course from the side! If you must transport people in the back, treat child locks with suspicion. It is possibly better to have your client get out of the car and run away than to have him or her attack you because it is impossible to get out of the car.

Office design

Similarly there are several useful rules that can be applied to the design of one's office to make incidents less likely to happen, or less dangerous if they do. For example:

1. The overall atmosphere of the office should be as conducive to relaxation and calming down as possible. Sometimes individuals like to have ornaments and plants in their office; which are good from the point of view of creating a calm and 'homely' atmosphere but on the other hand can be used as missiles. What one strives for is an environment which is reasonably calming, but at the same time does not have an excessive number of dangerous missiles to hand. It is surprising if one looks around one's office with a view to seeing what could be used as a missile, just how many there are.

2. If possible, sit yourself at least as near to the door as your client. There are two possible dangers: the first is that, by having the client further away from the door than you are, you will make him or her feel trapped; the other danger is, if you are further away from the door, that you run the risk of being taken hostage. Therefore, a reasonable rule of thumb is to have both people roughly equal distances from the door if possible. However, this may have to be overruled if it leads to an unnatural atmosphere (see 1 above).

3. If possible, have an 'easy area', consisting of about three chairs, away from the desk. This means you are able to move from the easy area to behind your desk, or vice versa. Thus, if you are talking to a client in the 'easy area' you have the option of saying words to the effect of 'this sounds pretty serious, I'd better just make a note of it', and moving behind your desk. Similarly you can move from behind the desk to the easy area. Sometimes, a simple move like this can stop the momentum of a situation building up.

4. If you know you are about to see a volatile client, see them in an office that is close to others, and preferably easy to supervise (for example, has glass panels in the door or has windows overlooking a thoroughfare). The function of this arrangement is that people will be aware if you are in trouble. It is of course important, and not by any means universal, that those people know what to do if they find you in trouble. This is mentioned under precautions.

5. If you regularly see potentially dangerous people in your office it may be possible to have an alarm fixed unobtrusively (say under the desk). If, administratively, it is too expensive to have such an arrangement, then there should at least be a telephone in the room. Some people do not like alarm buzzers, especially if the client is able to see them, because it is said to create an oppressive atmosphere. This may well be true if the button is visible, but there is no particular reason why it should be. In the eventuality of a serious incident arising most people would prefer to have a buzzer available than not to have one.

6. Ensure that the lock on your office door cannot be operated from the inside. Otherwise it is too easy for your client to take you captive and then barricade the door at leisure. Ideally one should have a deadlock, and ensure of course that the key is not in it.

Verbal behaviour

All the measures discussed so far have not involved even meeting the client. Many of them are, nevertheless, extremely important from the point of view of preventing an incident ever occurring, and should not be underestimated in that respect. However, there do arise situations where one has to deal with a person who is angry and aggressive. I shall tackle the skills necessary for dealing with such a situation under two headings, verbal behaviour and non-verbal behaviour. Some of the more important rules are as follows:

1. The general strategy is to attempt to:

(a) Calm the anger by displaying empathy, reflective listening, and all the general skills one has for soothing an individual. If one tries to solve the person's problems while he or she is still angry anything the therapist says will seem very naive, unsympathetic, etc. First, therefore, one must calm the person down to a state where they can at least begin to discuss the problem.

(b) One then needs to understand the problem, paraphrasing the context of what is said, and generally undertaking a problem-solving session, generating as many possible solutions as one can think of, and proceeding to establish which is the most likely to succeed. Only once the individual is slightly calmed, will he or she be amenable to this stage.

(c) Act to remedy the problem as far as possible, and as far as is appropriate.

It is very important to be able to judge whether one is in stage (a) or (b) because the transition from the first to the second can be very rapid. If one is trying to problem-solve while the person is still angry, this is likely to exacerbate the situation. On the other hand, if the angry person has gone on to the stage where he or she wishes to talk constructively about the problem and you are still simply displaying empathy, this too is likely to cause agitation.

2. If you are about to be assaulted as a 'probation officer', 'social worker', 'nurse', or any other role, in other words the assailant does not know you personally, but simply regards you as one of these professionals, it is important to personalize yourself. That is, you must enable the assailant to see you as a person rather than simply a role. It is one matter for an individual to assault, say, a social worker, but quite another to assault a named individual, with their own life going around them. How one does this is difficult to describe, outside the heat of the moment. Sometimes people will say something like: 'I wish you wouldn't shout like that because it frightens me, I'm a quiet person ...' and go on to say something about themselves and something about their background.

This is an important contrast with the situation which arises when a client knows you well and decides that, for whatever reason, he or she does not get on with you, or does not benefit particularly from seeing you. In this case, you are plainly doing no favours either to the client or yourself in continuing to see them, and might be well advised to transfer them to a colleague.

Just as one should personalize oneself, one should depersonalize the issue. In other words it is not your personal decision that, for example, the client cannot have what they are asking for, it is the policy of the organization, and it is a problem that you and they are going to have to sort out between you.

3. Ask for the required behaviour. For example if two people are fighting in front of you, there is no harm at all to be done by saying loudly (but reasonably calmly) and authoritatively 'stop hitting him', and simply repeating that until it is effective. The reason that many people do not try this is fear that they will not be obeyed. In that case, one has of course lost nothing.

4. In some violent situations one can see the escalation taking place. Rather like an aeroplane gaining momentum as it prepares to take off, one can see the situation gradually getting more and more out of hand. During this escalation phase one can try to regain control by asking questions about what the individual is concerned about. The advantage of this is that the person asking the questions is usually the one who is perceived as being in control, so long as the questions are answered. To ensure that they are answered, the questions need to be very closely tied to what the person is concerned about. For example, if a client's wife has left home, they can be 'did she take her clothes with her?' 'has she got any money?' and so on. Many clients find such questions simply too tempting, so they have to answer them. Repeated questioning like this can quickly put one back in control.

5. Again during the escalation phase one can try to regain control by shifting the situation. For example, saying 'let's go and have a cup of coffee and sort this out' (although this particular ploy can only be used early on in the build-up, for fear of having hot water thrown over you). Another example cited above was to utilize simply moving from behind the desk to the easy area in front of the desk or vice versa.

6. Some words seem to have a calming effect. 'We' is an excellent example of this because it implies a feeling of togetherness, the client and the professional working in unison. If you are working together, it does not make sense for him or her to hit you! Other words, especially 'no' and 'why' do exactly the opposite. People do not like hearing those words. They produce an emotional reaction.

7. For some reason, provocative phrases seem to spring to mind when one is under threat. Examples include: 'now don't be silly', 'just calm down', 'now pull yourself together'. Such phrases frequently seem to have exactly the opposite effect from what is intended; they act simply as a provocation. It is difficult to know how to avoid such phrases, except simply to be aware of the temptation of using them under stress, and try to immunize oneself against it.

Non-verbal behaviour

Non-verbal behaviour is sometimes considered to be more important than verbal communication: no matter whether an individual is psychotic, mentally handicapped or otherwise disturbed, most people respond to the cues of voice, posture, etc. (Argyle, 1984). As elsewhere, there are various points to bear in mind.

1. Sometimes it is appropriate to remain calm in the face of an aggressive person, but at other times this can be very agitating to him or her. One has to try to be sensitive to whether calmness is calming the aggressor or agitating him. In this field, one needs to be wary of general rules; however, it does seem to be generally reported that when it is oneself who is under threat, then it is usually a good idea to remain calm. When, alternatively, the aggressor is threatening a third party, and one is intervening on that person's behalf, then it is frequently a good idea to show explicitly that one realizes the seriousness of the situation and so to match the aggressor's aggression with concern, involvement, and an appreciation of the gravity of the situation. The general concept here is 'mood-matching'. However, one is matching the aggressor's aggression with an alternative form of arousal, and usually one would aim to have one's own arousal slightly less than the aggressor's. This would mean that although one is on the 'same wave-length' as the aggressor, one is modelling becoming progressively calmer.

2. Eye-contact can be aversive to many people, especially in potentially aggressive situations where it is sometimes interpreted as hostility. Therefore, one should beware of excessive eye-contact, or even eye-contact at all when a situation is developing into an aggressive and hostile one. Eye-contact tends to exaggerate whatever emotion is prevalent at the time; aggression may be exaggerated into violence. One ploy that is occasionally, but rarely, appropriate is that of taking notes. In an appropriate situation, this can come across as taking seriously what is being said, and giving the impression that some meaningful action will be taken about it. Simultaneously, of course, it avoids excessive eye-contact in a natural fashion.

3. If sitting, do not have the two chairs directly facing each other, as this can come across as a very hostile orientation once a situation begins to become aggressive. An angle of about 45 degrees is less threatening.

4. If possible, try to have seats of the same height for oneself and the client. Sometimes the person in the lower seat can seem in a dominant position, sometimes a subservient one, depending on a variety of other non-verbal cues that are given out.

5. Beware of standing in an aggressive situation. People are less likely to be hit when sitting down, but of course one does feel particularly vulnerable when sitting, in the sense that one is unable to duck or move out of the way as rapidly as one might if standing up.

6. If standing, try to adjust position to something approaching a 'friendly' angle to the would be aggressor. Most friendly men, for example, do not stand facing each other directly; this is a confrontational position and is usually best avoided. It is wiser in a heated interchange to stand at a slight angle to the other person.

7. A habitually violent person may have a wider body buffer zone than most, and it may therefore be appropriate to keep one's distance (McGurk et al., 1981). If anything, err on the side of being too far away from the individual, rather than be too close.

Miscellaneous points

There are a certain number of important considerations which do not fit under any other previous headings. These are:

1. Beware of one's own physical reactions if attacked. I have talked throughout this paper as though the professional is only likely to be the victim, rather than the aggressor. Some people react almost instinctively when they are hit, by hitting back. Remember that professionals are only allowed to use the minimum force necessary for their own safety.

2. Following an incident, do make sure that the laid down procedures of the organization are followed assiduously. Certainly document the incident thoroughly and inform the immediate senior. Sometimes people believe that because an incident is so well talked about and discussed, there is no need to record it formally. This is not so, all the procedures need to be followed.

3. Before entering a 'dicey' situation, give a moment's thought on how to handle it. Even two seconds thought is usually better than none. In fact, this general rule, 'keep thinking', is relevant throughout all and any violent incidents. There are few if any general rules that apply across all incidents; it is necessary to keep assessing the situation and judging for oneself how to react.

4. Beware of 'audience' effects. Frequently people will act violently to save face in front of others. Sometimes removing the audience, or removing the individual from the audience, can defuse a potentially aggressive situation. Remember that an audience may simply consist of one person.

5. Beware of the self-fulfilling prophecy. Sometimes discussing and having knowledge about a phenomenon seems magically to increase its incidence. In fact, most people reading this paper will be in the helping professions, and the purpose of learning about defusing violence is simply so that we can get on with our normal everyday job of helping other people. We are not aiming to be so preoccupied with violence that it inhibits this task, simply to be aware of some of the rules that govern when violent incidents occur, and how they might be avoided.

References

ARGYLE, M. (1984) **The Psychology of Interpersonal Behaviour** (4th ed.). Harmondsworth: Penguin

DAVIES, W.H. (1983) An analysis of inmate violence in a local prison. Unpublished PhD thesis, University of Birmingham

McGURK, B.J., DAVIES, J.D. and GRAHAM, J. (1981) Assaultive behaviour, personality, and personal space. **Aggressive Behaviour, 7,** 317-324

CONCLUDING COMMENTS

Kevin Howells and Clive Hollin

The papers presented in this volume cover a wide range of topics and types of offending behaviour. It is our view that they offer some grounds for optimism in the task of bringing clinical concepts and methods to bear on aggression and violence. Between them the papers reveal the not inconsiderable knowledge base available to the practitioner. This knowledge base, although incomplete, allows for a methodical and rational approach to the assessment of the violent individual and to the planning of behaviour change.

Ronald Blackburn's review of theories of aggression illustrates the relevance of social learning theory and, in particular, the important role of cognitive processes. Cognition is inseparable from the experience of anger and this particular emotion is the immediate antecedent of many, though not all, forms of violence. The identification of cognition and emotion as important features of some forms of violence is a significant step in two ways. First, as Blackburn's paper reveals, some theoretical debates at the heart of contemporary psychology, about the relationship between cognition and emotion (Lazarus, 1984; Zajonc, 1984) can be seen to be directly relevant to forensic work. Second, the whole range of cognitive psychotherapies, now becoming increasingly established as treatments of anxiety, depression and many other problems, can be seen to be of potential usefulness to the forensic clinician. Whether cognitive methods work as effectively with violence remains to be discovered by empirical research. The implication of this change of focus towards cognition and emotion is that forensic psychologists and psychiatrists may rediscover the many theoretical and clinical concerns they have in common with non-forensic workers.

How might psychiatric illnesses interact with the psychological and biological factors that cause violent behaviour? Robert Bluglass's paper suggests that formal psychiatric disorders such as depression and schizophrenia can affect the likelihood of violent behaviour occurring. Delusions, particularly of a paranoid nature, may be an important instigator. What Bluglass's discussion suggests is that violence in the mentally ill requires a multifactorial explanation, incorporating both features of the psychiatric disorder itself and also the myriad social and familial factors which trigger violent behaviour. As Bluglass suggests: 'It is a constellation of factors in dynamic interplay, occurring at a particular time, involving a unique sequence of events, which accounts for the cork being blown at a particular moment in time'. It follows that assessment and prevention require the identification of what factors make up the constellation for an individual, and a systematic attempt to remove their influence in the future.

Neil Frude, in his paper, addresses a particular form of violence - that directed towards children by adults. What is interesting and reassuring is that the model he derives has many consistencies with the cognitive-behavioural approach described by Ronald Blackburn. Frude effectively shows how a psychological model directs the clinician's attention to what needs to be assessed and to what should be the focus for therapeutic change. The aggressor's cognitive appraisals of the child's 'naughty' behaviour is clearly crucial, as is the angry arousal state which may have been induced by the child or by a range of other stressors. Models such as Frude's have a basis in theory and empirical research and this again suggests a comprehensive, systematic and multi-factorial intervention strategy whereby situations, appraisals, anger arousal and behaviour itself may all be targets for change.

Forensic clinicians typically deal with adult and adolescent offenders rather than with young children. There is an argument that long-term attempts to prevent violence will need to focus on changing violent behaviour in childhood before the full-blown pattern of adult violence has developed. Martin Herbert highlights the longitudinal consistency of aggressive and antisocial behaviour. Many violent children will also be violent adults. Herbert's analysis, again, brings us back to the need to identify the instigating situation and also the environmental consequences which may maintain or reinforce violent behaviour. Herbert concludes that 'there is little doubt that parents can be taught to use behavioural methods with their children and that for aggressive problems ... they are effective'. Whether effectiveness extends to preventing serious violence in late adolescence or adulthood is an important, largely unresearched, though clearly researchable, question. Herbert's concluding paragraphs alert us to a problem that runs throughout the other papers. Although treatment programmes for aggressive behaviour may be effective with clients who can be persuaded to co-operate and comply fully, such clients may form a minority in the populations with which the clinician works. As Herbert suggests, getting clients to the point of participating in assessment and treatment may be a major task in itself. Problems of lack of motivation for therapy will clearly need to be addressed in future clinical work with violent people.

Malcolm Gentry and Eugene Ostapiuk extend a behavioural analysis to a slightly older age group and to an institutional environment. These authors introduce the important distinction between <u>containment</u> and <u>treatment</u> of violence. A clear, specific and coherent containment policy, it is suggested, is a prerequisite for successful longer-term treatment. The obvious success in creating such a policy at Glenthorne YTC should not blind us to the fact that in many other settings such coherent policies may <u>not</u> exist (Drinkwater, 1982) and that confusion is common as to whether methods such as seclusion constitute a containment or a treatment method.

The case description provided by Gentry and Ostapiuk is a good example of the kind of detailed analysis of the problem and detailed setting of treatment goals which is required for changing violent behaviour. The planned move from external (institutional) to internal (self) control is clearly an essential feature of treatment in a closed setting and one that is carefully thought out at Glenthorne YTC.

The theme of 'containment' as opposed to long-term treatment, is continued in the final paper by William Davies. Virtually every professional working with violent people faces the possibility of being assaulted in the course of his or her contact with a client. Two issues arise: how to prevent violence, and how to respond to it once it arises. These are areas in which there is little theory or empirical work to which we can refer with confidence. William Davies provides some 'common-sense' pointers to good practice. It is our experience that, 'common-sense' though they may be, very few individual workers or organizations have given any systematic thought to prevention or management of a violent incident. It is to be hoped that William Davies' paper will stimulate further discussion and even some research into this neglected topic.

In summary, we believe these papers demonstrate that the clinical approach to aggression and violence is far from dead. The cognitive-behavioural model suggests systematic, detailed and comprehensive methods for assessing and changing violent behaviour which have some basis in psychological theory and empirical research. The full potential of such methods for the prevention of violence has yet to be explored.

References

DRINKWATER, J. (1982) Violence in psychiatric hospitals. In: M.P. Feldman (ed.) **Developments in the Study of Criminal Behaviour, Vol. 2: Violence.** Chichester: Wiley

LAZARUS, R.S. (1984) On the primacy of cognition. **American Psychologist, 39,** 124-129

ZAJONC, R.B. (1984) On the primacy of affect. **American Psychologist, 39,** 117-123

[illegible]

References

[illegible] (19[illegible]) [illegible] *Developments in the Study of Criminal Behaviour*, Vol. 2 [illegible]

[illegible]

[illegible]